Dedicated to:

Rachel Farnsworth
Sister-in-law
1980-2017

Because death is not the final answer.

"But thanks be to God! He gives us the victory through our Lord Jesus
Christ."
1 Corinthians 15:57

Contents

Made Known: How the God of the Universe Has Revealed Himself

Published in 2018

ISBN: 9781980215424

The cover photo was taken by the author at Grand Teton National Park.

Special thanks to Bonnie Straight for her help in editing.

Introduction

Can we know God? Many people, from all sorts of cultures and religious backgrounds have attempted to find God. Should we expect to be able to find answers?

This book is written for two groups of people. First, it's written for those who wonder what to believe about God, and even for people who are skeptical about religion. Perhaps you have deep questions. Perhaps you don't have answers yet. This book will hopefully meet you right where you're at, showing you that there are real answers to your questions.

Second, this book is written for those of you who are already followers of Jesus Christ. It is written to help you see that your faith rests on truth. There are things we can know about God. Those things can be used by God to strengthen your faith. I have been greatly aided by some Christian books that helped answer some of my questions. May this book help you! Maybe you can pass this book along to another person who is seeking or has questions.

It seems to me that, in our day and age, there is a growing distrust toward people who claim to have spiritual answers. It seems that lots of people assume that we *cannot* know things about God and that no one should suggest that one religion is any more valid than another. Along this line of reasoning, there seems to be a growing suspicion against anyone who would claim to know spiritual truth. Even though people allow us to believe things about God, they might look down on us for actually believing.

More and more, I hear people say things like, "I don't believe in God. I believe in science!" They might want you to believe that you must become a rational thinker who puts old superstitions behind you. To them, any religion is merely a man-made attempt to explain things.

Let me use an illustration. Have you seen the animated movie *Moana* yet? The people who made that movie invented a story about how the earth was created. They don't actually expect you to believe that story – they made up a fictional account. It works in an imaginary movie, but it doesn't explain what we see in real life.

You shouldn't believe the spiritual claims in *Moana* – it's admittedly fiction. But to some people, every spiritual explanation is fiction.

I don't think there needs to be a clash between science and truth from God. I think we can be both rational thinkers *and* people who seek truth from God. I believe this because I believe in a God who created science. Do you believe it's possible that there is a God who created the universe and did so in such a way that shows order? I think the reason we can study science is because we have a God who created in an orderly fashion.

But I'm getting ahead of myself already. I intend to show you the reasons why I believe in a creator God in chapter one.

For now, I want to urge you to be someone who will seek the truth. I want to urge you to do this because I believe in a God who reveals himself to those who seek him. Al Mohler, a leading theologian of today, said, "This God who really exists is truly knowable, but only because he has freely revealed himself to his human creatures."[1]

But we don't just have to listen to theologians. If my conclusions are correct in this book, God himself has promised that those who seek him will find him. Listen to what some verses in the Bible say about what will happen when you seek:

- Jesus said, "Ask and it will be given to you; seek and you will find; knock and the door will be opened to you. For everyone who asks receives; the one who seeks finds; and to the one who knocks, the door will be opened" (Matthew 7:7-8).
- Psalm 145:18 says, "The LORD is near to all who call on him, to all who call on him in truth."
- In Acts 17, the Apostle Paul talked about how God created and even picked the times and locations of our births. He went on to say in verse 26, "God did this so that they would seek him and perhaps reach out for him and find him, though he is not far from any one of us."

The purpose of this book is to encourage you to seek. I believe God will do his part when you seek and that you will find truth.

This book is set up so that each chapter builds on the previous one. In chapter one, I intend to show you that the mere fact that our universe exists shows us that there must be a supernatural creator.

In chapter two, I intend to show you how that creator has specifically revealed who he is. We are not left to wonder which god or gods created. God has made known to us who he is through the death and resurrection of Jesus Christ.

In chapter three, I want you to consider believing what Jesus believed about Scripture – that it is God's Word. Since Jesus had the authority to raise himself from the dead, I believe we should listen to whatever he says, and that means we should listen to what he says about the Bible. The God who created the universe, and us, has given us a book!

Then, in chapter four, we get to what is probably the most important part of the book. I do not want you simply to consider the truths in the first three chapters of this book. I want you to have a relationship with the God who made you, who sent Jesus for you, and who gave you his Word. In this way, you will not only have facts on your side, but also you will have a living, dynamic relationship with the God who created you. You can do more than know about God; you can know God.

1. Creation Reveals its Creator

"The heavens declare the glory of God; the skies proclaim the work of his hands."
Psalm 19:1

"She thinks I hung the moon!" It's an old saying, a saying a young man might use to describe how his girlfriend has fallen head-over-heels in love with him. According to this saying, this young woman is so taken by this young man that if you were to tell her that he put the moon in its place, she might actually believe you. Of course that would be ridiculous! None of us would take her seriously if she insisted on that point.

So who did hang the moon?

The very first verse of the Bible tells us. "In the beginning God created the heavens and the earth" (Genesis 1:1). But do we have good reason to believe this? Can we know who not only hung the moon, but also who created the universe?

We basically have two options to decide this question: either there is a natural or a supernatural explanation. (You could also say the answer is "both," but that includes the supernatural, so we'll just stick with our either/or scenario.) If we choose the *natural* answer, we would then expect the universe to have come into existence by the laws of science, even if we don't understand all of those laws yet.

If we choose the *supernatural* answer, we would then expect that there is something, or *someone*, above us – one who is able to do things which cannot be explained by natural law alone.

Admittedly, there is a bit of a difficulty here. A person could say, "There must be a natural explanation for the existence of the universe, we just don't know it yet." A person could say that for the rest of time.

But perhaps we do know enough right now to suggest the impossibility of the natural explanation of how the universe came into existence.

Let's start with a very simple attempt at that. Here it is: *nothing can't make something.*

I intend to back up that statement with some science in a moment. But for now, let's allow that simple statement to speak to us: *nothing can't make something.* Apart from God, who has the ability to create from nothing, when have we ever known anything to come from nothing? When has there ever been, naturally speaking, an "uncaused cause"? That would be unscientific.

In a debate, the well-known atheist Richard Dawkins once tried to explain how something could come from nothing. Here are his words:

> Of course it's counter-intuitive that you can get something from nothing. Of course common sense doesn't allow you to get something from nothing. That's why it's interesting. It's got to be interesting in order to give rise to the universe at all. Something pretty mysterious had to give rise to the origin of the universe, which is exactly what's meant by "nothing." But whatever it is, it's very, very simple.[1]

At this point in the debate, the audience started laughing, but the well-educated atheist couldn't figure out why. I think he has no answer as to why something could come from nothing, so instead he referred to "nothing" as "something."

For a very long time, people have tried to come up with answers as to how the universe came into existence without including God in the answer. For a very long time, they have come up against the same wall: *nothing can't make something.*

If nothing can't make something, perhaps the answer is that the universe has always existed. Along these lines, a person could simply say that he's using the Christian's argument about eternity, but just changing it a bit to suggest that the universe is eternal.

Does that work? I mentioned earlier that I would like to back up my simple statement with some science. Let's go there.

The first law of thermodynamics states that energy can neither be created nor destroyed. This explains that, naturally speaking, something doesn't come from nothing. (Note: when I say that energy cannot be created, I'm not talking about what happens at power plants, for example.

At a power plant, they can convert one kind of energy into a different kind of energy. But they always start with something – wind, solar energy, coal, water, etc. They do not create energy from nothing; they are in the business of energy conversion.)

The second law of thermodynamics describes how entropy always increases in closed systems. As former physics professor Danny Faulkner says, "Eventually, given enough time, all the energy of the universe would equalize."[2] A simple illustration of this would be placing a bucket of ice into one corner of a warm bath. Although starting at different temperatures, eventually, the ice would melt and the warm water would cool such that the temperature of the water in the tub would equalize. Because different parts of our universe are at different temperatures now, this law of thermodynamics demands that the universe has not infinitely existed, naturally speaking. If it were infinitely old, the temperature would be the same everywhere.

Why is any of this important? Here's why: the first law of thermodynamics precludes a natural explanation for the origin of the universe and the second law of thermodynamics precludes an eternally-existing universe.

Let me recap a bit here. There might seem to be two general solutions as to why the universe exists on a natural level. But both of them fail according to the laws of science. The first option would be to suggest that the universe came into existence by itself – this violates the first law of thermodynamics. The second option would be to suggest that the universe has always existed – this violates the second law of thermodynamics, because if the universe were infinitely old, the laws of entropy would demand that we would have already reached the equilibrium point (everything at the same temperature) at which point work as well as life would be impossible.

At this point, many people just throw their hands up in the air and say, "I guess we might never know the answer." But wait a moment. All I've done so far is to show that there is no *natural* explanation as to why the universe exists.

I realize that's a loaded statement, so I want to hang out there for a moment. Have I really, in a few short pages, defeated any attempt to explain the origin of the universe from a natural perspective?

Let's take a different angle at this. I said earlier that *nothing can't make something.* I want to appeal to your conscience for a moment. Do you or don't you believe that nothing can make something? I certainly don't. I've never seen it. Honestly, I don't know how it could happen. I cannot imagine something springing into existence without a cause.

This brings us to what philosophers call the "cosmological argument." One simple version of this argument is set forth by William Lane Craig. He says:

1. Whatever begins to exist has a cause.
2. The universe began to exist.
3. Therefore, the universe has a cause.[3]

The first part of this argument should be obvious to all of us. Otherwise, we're left with the idea of nothing making something. The second part of this argument may not seem as obvious, but it is much more rational, scientifically speaking, to suggest that the universe had a beginning than to suggest that it is eternal, for the reasons stated above. You could even say that suggesting an eternal universe delves into the supernatural realm anyway, as there would be no natural explanation as to why it has always existed.

The logical conclusion is that the universe has a cause. But what kind of cause?

So far, I hope you've seen that there can be no *natural* cause for the universe. This shouldn't leave us perplexed or resigned to the idea that we can't know anything about the origin of the universe. Rather, this should lead us to the following conclusion: *there is a supernatural explanation for the origin of the universe.*

As Faulkner said, "Science, if properly understood, does not preclude creation. In fact, the first and second laws of thermodynamics practically require it."[4]

Here's how the pastor-theologian Tim Keller puts it, "Again, because all natural beings have a cause, there must be some supernatural entity that exists without a cause, from which all has come."[5] He also says, quite succinctly, "Nothing cannot produce something."[6]

Or look at the words of Lee Strobel, a man who set out to prove Christianity wrong, only to be convinced by its truth. He said, "If there isn't a natural explanation and there doesn't seem to be the potential of finding one, then I believe it's appropriate to look at a supernatural explanation."[7]

Nothing can't make something.

At this point, I want to address a question which some of you might be thinking: "Doesn't this just shift the discussion back one step without answering it, because it doesn't explain where God came from? Where did God come from?"

It's a good question. I would simply like to show you what this question does in this discussion: it asks a *supernatural* question. To ask where I came from can be viewed as a natural question with a natural answer – I came from my parents. To ask where the universe came from is a natural question with a supernatural answer – God made it. To ask where God came from is a supernatural question with a supernatural answer – no one made him; he has always existed. So you see, it's perfectly legitimate to answer a natural question with a supernatural answer, especially since the laws of natural science demand it in the case of the origin of the universe. Likewise, it's okay to ask a supernatural question about God and to expect a supernatural answer. It's no problem for us to wonder how God can always have existed, since we know that to be a supernatural question.

This brings me back to my point: there can be no *natural* explanation of where the universe came from. There must be a *supernatural* explanation. Only when we include God in the discussion do we come to any possibility of an answer.

By the way, we should care about the question of our existence. "Where did the universe come from?" relates directly to the question, "Why am I here?" If you haven't wrestled with these questions, you're missing out. I am pleased to tell you that the answer to these questions involves a God who loves you and has good plans for your life. There is a supernatural reason why you exist.

An Argument for a Designer: Life

So far, we have looked into a fairly simple argument. The fact that something exists rather than nothing points us to a supernatural cause – God is the creator of the universe.

There's another powerful argument to consider when we look at how creation shows its creator. It has to do with the amazing intricacies of life. Why is it not only that things exist, but that some of those things – including us – can formulate thoughts and can reproduce after our own kinds?

In Charles Darwin's day, scientists knew that living beings were made out of cells. But the microscopes of his day were not nearly as powerful as those of our day. They knew relatively little about the cell. You can understand, then, why it might make sense to think of a cell as a simple structure. And, if the cell were a simple structure, it might be easy to conclude that it could come about by random chance. Given the right conditions, perhaps a cell could form itself in some "warm little pond," as Darwin implied in 1871 in a letter to Joseph Hooker.

But are cells simple structures?

In chapter 3 of the book *The Case for Faith* (which I recommend that you read, by the way), Lee Strobel interviews Walter L. Bradley, a former mechanical engineering professor who specialized in polymers and thermodynamics, eventually writing several books and articles on the origins of life. Bradley said that a cell, far from being a simple structure, is more like a "high-tech factory."[8]

Even the "simplest" forms of life known today are made up of millions of parts. I wouldn't call that very simple! In order for living things to live, these parts must interact with each other. In order to function, cells must have DNA, RNA, and proteins. All three of these things are incredibly complex and wouldn't work apart from each other. So, for the first cell to be alive – and you don't have life without cells – you need incredibly complex systems in place at the same time.

Let's just take one of those three and look at it a little more closely. Science has made tremendous advances in the last 30 years in regard to our understanding of DNA. Your DNA contains the information that made you. I use the word "information" because DNA uses what Bradley describes as a "four-letter chemical alphabet, whose letters combine in various sequences to form words, sentences, and paragraphs."[9] Sir David Attenborough calls it the "secret language of DNA" and the "book of life."[10]

It should be plain to see that DNA, which carries the instructions and information for all known living organisms, shows us a high level of design. Some scientists, many of whom made their decisions about the origin of life before we came to understand DNA, would like to tell you that the information encoded in DNA came about by chance.

Let's use an illustration to see how realistic it is to ascribe this to chance. Picture a lake in which the waves make markings on the soft sand of the beach. You could analyze those markings and look for patterns. By random chance, you might be able to find some small patterns in the ripples in the sand, even repeated patterns. But you would never expect to find *information*. Imagine if you were a scientist studying these markings on the sand and you showed up one morning to see written in the sand, "I love you, Keith," inside of a heart. Would you shriek out in joy and say,

"The waves did it! They made a message!'"? Or would you assume that a person came while you were gone and wrote that message?

The instructions encoded in DNA are often compared to a book. Inside your DNA book is the information that determines what your physical body will be like.

Here's one important thing about books: they have authors. I've never read a book written by no one. I've never read a book written by random chance, or by the waves of a lake, or by the forces inside a warm little pond. The information stored in DNA points us to someone wise enough to write that information.

Design implies a designer.

To illustrate this point, I want to use a famous analogy, called "The Watchmaker Analogy." Imagine walking in a desert – I don't know why you're there, but just stay with me here. You see nothing around you but miles and miles of sand. Then, picture yourself catching the reflection of the sun off of something in the sand. You go over and pick up the object – a watch. Would you say to yourself, "Wow! What are the chances that, over billions and billions of years, the wind and the elements of the earth formed this watch?" Imagine then, to your surprise, to see that this watch is still keeping the correct time. Would you still think that there was no intent or design behind the watch? Of course not. The logical mind would know that this watch was designed for a purpose. Why would we look at our universe, or at an intelligent being like you or me, and suggest that we were not designed for a purpose?

It won't work to suggest a time when life was simpler – perhaps to say that, yes life now is complex, but maybe it was simpler back then and didn't need design. That won't work because we now know that cells are complex, not simple. Cells must do multiple things in order to live and to reproduce.

As if this weren't enough, I'd like to apply the principle I started out with in this chapter: even if we were to agree that living cells could form themselves if given the right conditions, why were there any conditions at all in which there was matter?

Without God in this process, you're left with the unanswerable questions of both where the matter and where the information came from. There must be a supernatural answer.

Design implies a designer.

I read an argument recently from an atheist whose conclusion was that there is no convincing evidence to show us that there is a god. A person could suggest that all we see is the natural, that we never see evidence of the supernatural.

I would like to suggest to you that the existence of all we see and the design of life are two very strong evidences of a creator.

The Answer Was with You All the While

In 1985, the rock band Survivor released a song about a man who took for granted his friendship with a woman. He was "always reachin'" while she was right there in front of him. She was the answer, but he was unable to see what should have been obvious. But when he finally looked into her eyes, he realized "The search is over" – that's the title of the song. In the next line, he says, "You were with me all the while."

According to a 2017 poll done by the American Bible Society, the average household in America has about four Bibles. Could it be that the answer has been right with you all the while, in your home? Does the Bible have answers in our quest for the origin of the universe? (Note: In chapter 3, I intend to show you why I think the Bible is the word of God. For the purposes of this chapter, I want to go to the Bible to see if it will help us understand the origin of the universe.)

As I said earlier, if you were to pick up a Bible, you could see the very first verse in it says, "In the beginning God created the heavens and the earth" (Genesis 1:1). In the first two chapters, we see some specific information about how God made not only the stuff of the earth, but human beings as well. We're told in Genesis 1:27 that man and woman were made in the image of God. In Genesis 2:7, we see that the first man, Adam, was a special creation formed by God from the dust of the earth. In that same chapter, the first woman, Eve, was also a special creation formed by God.

If that's true, then there is not only order, but also purpose behind your existence. Which one makes more sense: that you owe yourself to random chance or that you were designed on purpose and therefore have a purpose?

I mentioned above an atheistic argument which says there is no convincing evidence to show us that there is a god. What does the Bible say about that?

There's a powerful passage in the book of Psalms which gives us some evidence. The Psalms were, you could say, a hymnbook for God's followers during the last millennium before Jesus was born. One of those psalms was a song of praise for the God who has revealed himself to his people. Psalm 19:1-4a says,

> [1] The heavens declare the glory of God; the skies proclaim the work of his hands.
> [2] Day after day they pour forth speech; night after night they reveal knowledge.
> [3] They have no speech, they use no words; no sound is heard from them.
> [4] Yet their voice goes out into all the earth, their words to the ends of the world.

According to verses 1-2, the heavens (that is, the heavenly bodies like the stars, sun, and moon) and the skies have a message for us. Every day and night, they have something to tell us. Even though, like it says in verse 3, they have no speech, use no words, and no sound is heard from them, their message rings out to the ends of the world, as it says in verse 4. (Interestingly, when verse 4 is quoted in the New Testament in Romans 10:18, and therefore in a different language, the word for "voice" is a word than can also refer to a musical tone. Along those lines, we could say that the heavens and the skies speak to us as in a musical language.)

God's creation has been proclaiming the glory of God to you ever since you were born. For your whole life, the constant message of that which God created has proclaimed to you that his hands made it all. There is a message from the skies: there is a creator!

Does God really expect us to hear the voice of the skies? Yes he does. Romans 1:20 says, "For since the creation of the world God's invisible qualities—his eternal power and divine nature—have been clearly seen, being understood from what has been made, so that people are without excuse."

Do you see what that verse says? The *invisible* qualities of God have been *clearly seen* through what has been made. Creation testifies to us that God is the creator. This testimony is so powerful that, according to this verse, we are left without excuse if we deny this truth. None of us could stand before God on judgment day and say, "Well, if you would have left me with a little more evidence, I might have believed!" We have enough evidence. The heavens declare it. It is clearly seen and understood through what has been made. God has revealed this truth to us.

But some people suppress this truth. In fact, that's what we see in Romans 1:18, two verses before the verse I just quoted. According to Romans 1:19, there are things that may plainly be known about God. But verse 18 says that some people "suppress the truth by their wickedness." There are some people who drown out the testimony of the heavens in order to come up with some other reason why there is no creator.

Why would anyone do that? Why would anyone look at what is created and come up with some explanation that leaves God out of the picture?

According to Michael Behe, some people perhaps just don't want there to be a god. He said, "Many people, including many important and well-respected scientists, just don't *want* there to be anything beyond nature."[11]

That might be the crux of the matter. We all come into this with bias. If there is no god, then perhaps we have the right to live our lives simply how we want. If God exists, then we have a responsibility to him.

So which one is it? Is there any way we can tell?

What does the evidence say? I hope what you've seen in this chapter is that there are good, scientific, logical reasons to believe that there is a God who created the universe. And the universe itself testifies to us that God created. As Lee Strobel says, "God makes sense of the universe's origin."[12] I would say that there is no other explanation that makes sense of the universe's origin.

A Personal Story

To me, this isn't merely an academic or philosophical topic. The question of how anything came into existence was perhaps the most important, and difficult, question for me in the early years of my spiritual journey. I'll mention some other questions later, but this question stands out as the most important.

As a sophomore in high school, I prayed to receive Jesus Christ as my Savior and Lord. There was a very strong sense in my heart that I should do so. In one sense, I never looked back – I have walked with him ever since then. But in another sense, my heart was ahead of my mind at that point in time. I still had questions.

Soon after I prayed to receive Jesus, I started asking questions, difficult questions. I thought that if this relationship with Jesus is legitimate, there should be answers to the real questions of life. I made it my goal to ask the most difficult questions I could ask. I wanted answers. I wanted them not only to be able to give to other people, but also because I wanted to know. I wanted to know if I was tricking myself into believing in something that wasn't true.

As I implied above, the most difficult question for me had to do with origins. Where did we come from? Where did the universe come from? I began to wonder, "What if my prayers don't make it past the ceiling?" I started to ask the question if it was legitimate to believe in a creator. I started, kind of like the atheist I mentioned above, to wonder why there wasn't more evidence for the supernatural. I had committed my heart to God. Why wouldn't he give me some undeniable sign that he really existed so that my mind would be satisfied, too? Without evidence that satisfied my mind, could my heart truly believe?

If you haven't noticed by now, I'm a rational thinker. I *love* math – it makes sense and you can prove that it makes sense. Along those same lines, I really enjoy science. I have a degree in civil engineering. I like it when we can point to concrete solutions. (Civil engineers will understand that pun. My wife will probably roll her eyes at it.)

My mind was troubled as I grasped for a solution. This became not just a theological question, but a question that shouted inside of me, demanding an answer. Could I ever know if God exists? Would I just have to take it on "blind faith"? Could I take it on "blind faith" if my mind wasn't convinced?

But at the same time, it didn't make sense to me that there were only natural answers. Even as I struggled to find supernatural answers, I was never convinced that the atheistic proposal was any better. Although I wanted a supernatural sign, I didn't assume that my lack of seeing a sign was proof against God. My mind wasn't yet convinced in either direction.

Then, one evening, I got my answer. You could call it a sign. You could call it a "Hallelujah" moment. I prefer to call it an answer that was with me all the while.

I had three good friends in high school who lived within walking distance of my house. Often times I would stay at one of their houses until after sunset. On those walks home, I was often struck by the beauty of the moon against the backdrop of the stars. I still am. It's amazing to me that this huge mass floats in space at just the right distance to control our tides here on earth. It's beautiful when it's all lit up. It's a little mysterious when you can only see a sliver of it.

One night in particular, as I contemplated the moon, I thought to myself, "I didn't make that. Neither did my parents. Or their parents." (I could go on from there, but I think you get the point.) At that point, I realized that, because nothing can't make something, there must be a supernatural explanation. At that moment, for maybe the first time in my life, I heard the message of the skies, proclaiming they are the work of God's hands.

For me, that evidence came by contemplating the moon. For others, it might come through thinking about the miracle of a baby or the beauty of nature. For others, it might be the amazing intricacies at the molecular or atomic level. I believe God has given us evidence.

From there, the logic is easy. The God who made the moon also made us. The Bible tells us, "… all things have been created through him and for him" (Colossians 1:16). I became convinced that not only did God make me, but also that he has good plans for me. The best life for me is the one in which I live for him.

God hung the moon. I came to know that truth that night, and my mind fell more in love with God.

2. The Resurrection of Jesus Shows the Power of God

"I want to know Christ—yes, to know the power of his resurrection..."
Philippians 3:10a

In chapter one of this book, I showed that there must be a supernatural explanation for the existence of our universe. God exists.

But which God exists? Is it the God of Christianity? Or the gods of Hinduism? Or the Flying Spaghetti Monster (seriously, there's a church for this one – it's called "Pastafarianism")?

Can we know? If God created, like I asserted in chapter one, has he left any evidence as to who he is? Or are we frustratingly left with vague non-answers? In the fictional movie *Moana*, there is lots of evidence of the supernatural: water that interacts with people, a demi-god named Maui who can shape-shift into all sorts of animal forms, and the imposing goddess Te Fiti who is a force to be reckoned with. But has the real God of the universe left his fingerprints in our world, telling us specifically who he is?

Let's start off with an illustration. Picture yourself traveling in the 19th century in what is now central Arizona and coming across a large crater in the earth. You might wonder, "How did this big hole get here?" You might come up with some ideas. Perhaps some ancient civilization dug the hole. But the crater is awfully big. Or maybe the crater is like other craters you've heard of and was caused by volcanic activity. But there doesn't appear to be a volcano in the immediate area. Or maybe this crater was caused – and this might sound ridiculous to some – by an incoming object from space. You might have been laughed at by some people to suggest such a cause... except that this is exactly how this crater was formed. We call it "Meteor Crater" today. The evidence bears out the truth – that a meteorite barreled into the ground and dug out the crater. In this case, you could investigate the evidence and come out with solid information about how the crater was formed.

So, getting back to God, has he left any evidence such that we can know who he is? I believe he has. I believe that evidence comes to us in the form of the resurrection of Jesus Christ. We're told in John 1:18 that God sent Jesus for the very reason that God would be made known to us. I believe the resurrection does this in a very powerful way.

The message of Christianity is that Jesus Christ is the Son of God who lived a perfect life and offered himself as the perfect sacrifice for our sins so that anyone who believes in him can have complete forgiveness and eternal life. But, according to the Bible, Jesus didn't stay dead. On the third day, he was raised back to life – that's the resurrection.

If the resurrection is true, it is a complete vindication of Jesus Christ being the Son of God and we would then have evidence for the God in whom we should believe. The God of the Bible sent his Son, the Lord Jesus Christ, to our world to save us.

The Bible tells us, in Acts 17:31, that God will "judge the world with justice by the man he has appointed." The "man" in that verse is Jesus. In the next part of that verse it says, "He [God] has given proof of this to everyone by raising him from the dead." I find this fascinating, because the people to whom those words were first spoken lived in Athens, Greece (about 780 miles by sea or 1850 miles by land away from Jerusalem) and about two decades after the resurrection occurred. Yet the resurrection of Jesus is said to be "proof," not just to them, but "to everyone." That word "proof" is the same word used in the Bible for faith. According to this verse, the resurrection of Jesus is something on which any person – even those who didn't see the resurrection – can base their faith. It tells you which God you will meet when you die. If the Bible is correct on this point, the resurrection of Jesus tells us which God exists.

Jesus himself told the people of his day to go where the evidence would lead. He said, "... believe the miracles, that you may know and understand that the Father is in me, and I in the Father" (John 10:38b). His resurrection from the dead was the biggest miracle during his time on earth. It was done in order that we would believe in him.

At this point, I know what you might be thinking: "Prove it."

I would like to suggest to you that there is something almost like a crater to which we can point. The resurrection of Jesus Christ from the dead has left such an impact on our world that it sets him apart, not as one god among many, but as God the Son, part of the Trinity worshiped in Christianity.

First, let's analyze this spiritual crater left by the resurrection of Jesus from the dead.

By any account, Jesus had an astonishing impact on this world. At the present time, it's estimated that there are over two billion Christians in the world. That is to say, over two billion people claim that Jesus died and rose again.

But the crater left by Jesus' resurrection isn't only a modern-day phenomenon. Soon after his resurrection, Christianity spread rapidly. As is clearly seen by the letters of the Apostle Paul and the book of Acts in the Bible, people were worshiping Jesus all over the vast Roman Empire within a relatively short time span. And this all happened in a time when Christians were persecuted by both Romans and Jews – the Jews immediately started persecuting Christians and the Romans followed suit within 35 years after Jesus' resurrection. People didn't become Christians in those days to win popularity contests – in fact, it cost many of them their lives. I mention this because it should be clear to see that many people really believed the story of the resurrection.

This story of the resurrection of Jesus comes to us from his closest followers, the apostles. The apostles were a group made up of Jesus' disciples (people who knew him very well), as well as two people, James and Paul, who were contemporaries of Jesus, but didn't believe in him until shortly after his resurrection.

Here's the important question: *should we believe the story of the resurrection of Jesus Christ from the dead as given to us by the apostles?* If they got the story right, we should all believe in Jesus. If they got it wrong, then their story has deceived billions of people and it should be rejected. Josh McDowell wrote, "… the resurrection of Jesus Christ is either one of the most wicked, vicious, heartless hoaxes ever foisted upon people, or it is the most important fact of history."[1] Historically speaking, the story of the resurrection of Jesus is so important that we all really should consider whether it is true or false.

Again, back to the evidence – is there any evidence to suggest that Jesus did rise from the dead?

We know there is a crater. The story of Jesus has left a huge impact. What is it that best describes how that impact was made?

What I want to do with the rest of this chapter is to analyze the options we have. Either Jesus did or didn't rise from the dead. I want to investigate. I want you to see what makes the most sense. My approach will be first to look at alternative theories to the resurrection – theories which would lead a person to deny the resurrection. Then, I will give my case as to why the resurrection really happened.

First, let's analyze the theories which would discredit the resurrection. Since the story of Jesus has made such an impact in this world, in order to discredit Christianity one would need to come up with at least one good theory – a believable theory – that explains away the evidence of the resurrection. If no theory can adequately explain away the evidence and if belief in the resurrection does explain the evidence, then the reasonable conclusion would be that Jesus did rise from the dead.

Some of these alternative theories overlap a little bit. I have attempted to categorize them in such a way as to cover all the possible theories.

Alternative Theory #1: The Apostles Were Deceived

According to this theory, the apostles sincerely believed what they said and wrote, but they were mistaken. On one level, this theory makes sense because, after following Jesus for years, you can imagine that they wanted him to be a messenger from God. His death would have been a humiliating defeat for his followers. So it follows that the apostles would have been prone to believe that Jesus rose from the dead even if he didn't do so. As one person said to me, "They needed Jesus to be alive again."

Does this theory make sense? Could this group of people have been deceived like this?

In order to answer yes to that question, we would have to figure out a story in which they were all deceived in a similar way, because their stories of Jesus are similar. What could that deception look like?

One suggestion is that the tomb is not empty, that the followers of Jesus forgot where Jesus was buried and then came up with the solution that he must have risen from the dead. But this suggestion is woefully inadequate. Surely, someone amongst the group of followers would have remembered the correct tomb. If not, all it would have taken to squelch this young movement would be for one of the Jews or the Romans to find the correct tomb and produce the body. The dead body of Jesus would have been the nail in the coffin for Christianity, so to speak.

Another suggestion is that the apostles were hallucinating. Since theirs was a religious journey, some people have speculated that their minds were open to visions. Since they wanted Jesus to be alive, they would have been readily influenced, even by false visions. But this suggestion, too, is woefully inadequate due to the number of people who saw Jesus alive. In 1 Corinthians 15 (a very important passage, which I'll mention repeatedly in this chapter), it says in verse 6 that the resurrected Jesus appeared to more than 500 people at the same time. The Apostle Paul even added there that most of those people were still living, as if to say, "You can ask them. They saw him." I've never heard of such a mass hallucination, have you? Not only that, but also many of the people who saw Jesus alive after his death had the privilege of touching him or eating with him. In John 20:27, Jesus told the Apostle Thomas (one of the 12 disciples) to touch his hands and side. This caused Thomas, who was beforehand a skeptic, to believe in Jesus, saying to him, "My Lord and my God!" (John 20:28). Similarly, in John 21:13, we're told that Jesus gave bread and fish to seven of his followers. Hallucinations don't serve you meals. Finally, the apostles also testified, in Acts 1:9, that they saw Jesus as he was taken up into heaven.

Due to the large number of people who saw Jesus alive and due to the fact that no dead body could be found, it seems very unlikely that any theory of the apostles being deceived could hold water.

But what if it's more vicious than that? What if the apostles weren't deceived, but were themselves the deceivers?

Alternative Theory #2: The Apostles Were Lying
According to this theory, the apostles knew full well that Jesus remained dead, but they kept the story going by claiming that he had risen from the dead. Along these lines, the apostles' motive would be to gain fame as people who started what is now a worldwide movement.

Is it reasonable to suggest that the followers of Jesus knowingly perpetuated this lie? To answer that question, I want to look at three other questions.

1) Could they pull it off?
Even if the apostles wanted to keep this movement going by pretending that Jesus was still alive, could they have pulled it off? Like I said above, all it would have taken was for one person to find the dead body of Jesus and the whole movement would die. This movement spread rapidly, and it did so right in the heart of where Jesus was killed. The Romans and the Jews both had major motivation to squelch this movement. We know from the writings of the Bible and from history that

they tried to squelch the movement. It would have been an astonishing feat for this group of lying apostles to outwit the much more powerful authorities of their day. Are we to suggest that, not only did the apostles pull off this hoax, but also that all of them kept professing their lie to their graves, even under intense interrogation and threats of imprisonment and death? They would have had ample opportunity to recant their lie. This leads to the next question.

2) What would the apostles stand to gain if they kept this lie going?

According to this alternative theory, the apostles had fame to gain if they kept the message of Jesus alive, even if Jesus himself was still dead. But is fame what they got?

History tells us what happened to them as they spread this story across the world – they were persecuted. Counting the 11 remaining disciples (taking Judas, the betrayer, out of the discussion) as well as James and Paul, the two apostles I mentioned above, all but one of them were killed for their faith. The one who wasn't killed, John, didn't have it much easier – he was imprisoned and tortured for his faith.

At the time of Jesus' death, the apostles were pictured as people who doubted Jesus and hid out of fear that they would face the same punishment as he did. One of them, Peter, even denied three times that he knew Jesus. Paul, one of the apostles who came to believe in Jesus after his resurrection, started out as one who persecuted those who believed in Jesus – he of all people knew the danger of being a follower of Jesus.

Are we to believe, then, that these people, knowing it to be a lie, spread the message of the resurrection of Jesus to the known world, knowing it would cost them dearly?

In chapter 5 of *More Than a Carpenter* by Josh McDowell (which I suggest you read, by the way – it was tremendously helpful in my early faith journey), McDowell says,

> Now if the resurrection didn't take place (i.e., was false), the disciples knew it… Therefore these eleven men not only died for a lie – here is the catch – but they knew it was a lie. It would be hard to find eleven people in history who died for a lie, knowing it was a lie.[2]

3) Is this theory in line with what we know of the apostles?

Even a quick overview of the writings of the New Testament would show you that lying is a sin in the eyes of God. Should we suggest that a group of liars perpetuated a story which repeatedly says we shouldn't lie?

William Lane Craig concludes that the theory of lying apostles is "morally implausible."[3] The picture of their lives is a picture of people genuinely devoted to the one they considered to be their Lord and Savior, following his teachings. In contrast, this alternative theory suggests we should brand them as wicked deceivers.

Along these lines, Craig tells us that "this explanation has been completely given up by modern scholarship."[4]

So far, it doesn't seem to be convincing to suggest that the apostles were either deceived or the deceivers. But there are still some other options to deal with.

Alternative Theory #3: Jesus Didn't Actually Die on the Cross (The Swoon Theory)

According to this theory, Jesus was nailed to a Roman cross, but he faked his death and was restored to health after being placed in a cool tomb for a few days.

There are two major problems with this theory.

1) It is so very unlikely that a person could have pulled this off.

Before he was crucified, Jesus was whipped severely. Many died from such a flogging. Then, he was nailed to a cross in such a way that death would come from asphyxiation or heart failure.

In chapter 11 of his book *The Case for Christ*, Lee Strobel interviewed Dr. Alexander Metherell. (I suggest you read that chapter, or even the entire book for that matter.) In that chapter, Dr. Metherell convincingly tells us why it would have been impossible for a person to endure the flogging and crucifixion.[5]

For one, Jesus would likely have been in critical condition from the flogging alone. Even without the following torture of the cross, a person would have needed immediate medical attention in order to survive the whipping.

Following that, the crucifixion was a particularly brutal form of capital punishment. It was designed to kill a person by making it difficult, then impossible, to breathe. Due to the positioning of a body on the cross, with hands/wrists and feet painfully nailed on it, a person would struggle to lift his body in order to complete the process of inhaling and exhaling. In physical agony from pushing up on the nails, a person would slowly lose his ability to expand and contract his diaphragm, with the eventual result of suffocation or heart failure.

All four Gospels in the Bible give a description of this kind of a death. But there's more. As his body was left to hang on the cross after his last breath, the soldiers waited for the two thieves who were crucified next to Jesus to die. To speed up their deaths, their legs were broken, making breathing almost impossible. But when they came to Jesus, they saw him hanging lifelessly and decided instead to pierce his side with a spear, apparently to make sure he wasn't faking it. (Not that a person could really fake such a death, as slumping downward on the cross would make breathing impossible.) When they pierced his side, according to John 19:34, there was "a sudden flow of blood and water." Dr. Metherell describes how that would happen due to the spear piercing both lung and heart, releasing a clear fluid which had built up during the ordeal of the cross. In conclusion, Dr. Metherell authoritatively said, "There was absolutely no doubt that Jesus was dead."[6]

The Romans were good at killing people on crosses. It would be incredibly hard to believe that a person could have submitted himself to their method of capital punishment, yet come out alive. But even if Jesus did, there's another huge problem.

2) The story of Christianity isn't that Jesus survived the cross; it's that he died and rose again. William Lane Craig said,

> Even if Jesus had survived, his appearing to the disciples half-dead and desperately in need of medical attention would not have evoked their worship of him as Lord. The conviction of the earliest disciples was that Jesus rose gloriously and triumphantly from the grave, not as one who had managed to barely escape death.[7]

But let's suggest, for a moment, that Jesus did survive the cross and that the apostles were duped into believing that he had been raised from the dead. That still wouldn't explain why they said they saw him ascend into the sky in Acts 1:9. As they described that scene, they said two angelic figures told them that Jesus was taken into heaven and would come back again (Acts 1:11). Now that would be very hard to fake!

An apparent, or faked, death would not lead the apostles to go throughout the world and proclaim that Jesus died and rose again.

Or, let's suggest for a moment that the apostles were in on the story – that they helped Jesus fake his death. This suggestion falls short for reasons mentioned above. Jesus certainly died on the cross. If he didn't, the movement would have been squelched by finding Jesus' body, dead or alive. Also, neither Jesus nor the apostles bear any indication of being wicked deceivers.

We're running out of possibilities here. There's another one that is being suggested as a possibility to explain everything away.

Alternative Theory #4: It's All a Legend

According to this theory, Jesus was simply a good man, a powerful teacher, and a religious leader – but fictional stories about him grew and grew after his death. This theory is perhaps the most convenient way to reject the idea that Jesus is God the Son, because it still allows people to hold him in high regard as a teacher, but without the need to worship him or follow him.

In order for this theory to work, there would need to be a certain amount of time to pass in between Jesus' death and the made-up legend that became associated with him.

Let me use an illustration to explain this. I am a Minnesota Twins fan. The Twins had a brutal year in 2016, finishing with the worst record in major league baseball, by far. Imagine if I decided to start a legend which says that the Twins won the World Series that year. All you would have to do in order to squelch that story would be to talk to Twins fans. Even if we didn't have the internet or newspapers, you could simply ask Minnesotans how the Twins did in 2016, and they would tell you: they did awful! This same line of reasoning applies all the way back to the year 1991, when the Twins actually did win their last World Series title. If I suggested any year between 1992 and 2017, it would be very easy to disprove me.

Legends need time in order to develop, or else they can easily be disproven.

So, what kind of timeline are we dealing with in regard to the resurrection of Jesus? Some people might try to pull a fast one on you, talking about how the dates when the books of the Bible were written are much, much later than when the events happened. Although some of the books weren't written until about 60 years after Jesus' death, many of them were written much sooner.

In fact, there's one really important passage in this regard – the one I mentioned earlier: 1 Corinthians 15. In that passage, the Apostle Paul talks about the Gospel, a message he received and passed along. Paul explains in verses 3-8 how Jesus died for our sins, was buried, was raised to life, and then that he appeared to a bunch of people – more than 500 of them! – and then appeared to the apostles, including Paul himself. Gary Habermas brilliantly walks through the timeline of 1 Corinthians 15, showing us how very early its content came about. (I encourage you to do an internet search of "Gary Habermas Resurrection" to find a video in which he walks through this timeline.) The short story of it is that, due to the historical markers within 1 Corinthians, we can easily place the resurrection of Jesus and the written story of his resurrection within 25 years of each other. With a little more digging, we can see that it's more likely that the details of the resurrection were arranged into a creed, perhaps even within months, and the story was widely dispersed within six years of the resurrection. That's not enough time for legend to creep in.

We're dealing with history here. Although we might like to have videotape evidence of the resurrection, we won't get that. What we can piece together – and we can do this with the story of the life, death and resurrection of Jesus better than we can with almost any other ancient historical figure – is that, from soon after his death and resurrection, the story of his death and resurrection was quickly circulated.

Not only do we have the eyewitness accounts of the apostles – as if that weren't enough – but also we have other historians from near the time of Jesus telling us about Jesus. Within 100 years, we have historians like Josephus and Tacitus telling us about Jesus. Tacitus tells us how there was a movement based on a crucified Christ, a movement full of people who were willing to die for him.[8] Pliny the Younger tells of how Christians would chant "in honor of Christ as if to a god."[9] Even without what the Bible says, history clearly tells us that a movement was started in which people believed that Jesus rose from the dead.

Taken together with the timeline of the Bible, it's clear that this is not a legend. If legendary tales were falsely added to a true story of Jesus as simply a moral teacher, there would have been many eyewitnesses who could have squashed the legend. The actual eyewitnesses tell a much different story. The best explanation is that people really saw Jesus alive after his death. Josh McDowell said, "A believer in Jesus Christ today can have complete confidence, as did the first Christians, that his faith is based, not on myth or legend, but on the solid historical fact of the risen Christ and the empty tomb."[10]

Alternative Theory #5: There Never Was a Jesus of Nazareth

According to this theory, the story of the life of Jesus is more than a legend – it's a myth. The appeal of this theory is that it easily explains how the resurrection need not have happened. However, the weight of history makes this theory impossible. A beginning glance at history will show you that it was not only the followers of Jesus who wrote about him. As I mentioned above, multiple historical accounts – even some written from people who would not call themselves Christians – tell us about a real man named Jesus who led a spiritual movement. Just to recap a few of those names, we have historical accounts of Jesus from Josephus, Tacitus, and Pliny the Younger.

This theory is merely a grasping at straws and barely even deserves to be mentioned, except to say that it is not rational to deny the resurrection by suggesting that Jesus never lived.

There's one more alternative theory to deal with. After what I've already written about history, you should be able to see the inadequacy of this final alternative theory.

Alternative Theory #6: It Wasn't Jesus Who Died on the Cross

According to this theory, Jesus was such a man of God that God himself intervened and made a body swap so that Jesus wasn't crucified – it was, instead, someone who merely looked like him.

This theory is probably made most famous by the Koran, the holy book of Islam. In Surah 4:157, it says of those who thought they killed Jesus, "Yet they slew him not, and they crucified him not, but they had only his likeness."[11]

Other versions of this theory suggest that God made things right at the time of the crucifixion by taking Jesus up to heaven and making Judas Iscariot, the one who betrayed Jesus, endure the cross.

The question here is: why should we believe these theories?

In the case of the Koran, there were no eyewitnesses to this body swap. We would simply be left to take Muhammad's word for it, about 600 years after the resurrection. He claimed that God gave him messages in a cave. Unlike the apostles, I would suggest that Muhammad stood to gain a great deal of earthly benefits if his teachings were followed – he was both a religious and a military leader, whereas most of the Christian apostles were killed for their testimony.

I don't want to take much space right now to contrast Islam and Christianity. However, I will say one thing: the Christian story is based on multiple eyewitness accounts, whereas Islam's story of the cross is based on one man's claimed vision about 600 years after the event. I am glad to believe the Christian story, the story that passes the historical test of verification. For a more detailed treatment of Islam versus Christianity, I recommend *Seeking Allah, Finding Jesus* by Nabeel Qureshi.

Ironically, Muhammad pointed out one thing that I have tried to show you: the story of the resurrection of Jesus changed the world. The fact that this story made it about 600 years to Muhammad and another 1400 years to us shows us that something powerful happened that day.

Do Any of These Alternative Theories Work?

After walking through these alternative theories, we must question whether any of them stand on solid ground. Again, because the story of the resurrection of Jesus from the dead is such an important story, historically speaking, we must consider whether it is true.

I would suggest that none of these alternative theories come close to bearing the weight of their own conclusions. I have tried to be thorough. I have investigated the alternative claims. I challenge you to look into these matters for yourselves. What you'll find is that there is no alternative theory that holds water.

What if the story is true? If Jesus really died and was raised to life again, then we have eternal life to look forward to if we believe in him. Romans 10:9 says, "If you declare with your mouth, 'Jesus is Lord,' and believe in your heart that God raised him from the dead, you will be saved."

Can we build a positive case for the resurrection of Jesus? So far, I have shown you that the story of the resurrection changed the world and that no alternative theory explains the evidence. I would now like to show you evidence that the resurrection really did happen. I have mentioned some of these reasons already. I would now like to build them together into a positive case for the resurrection.

The Best Theory: Jesus is Alive Again!

The apostles claimed that Jesus of Nazareth was put to death on a Roman cross and was buried in a tomb. But they also claimed that he was raised to life. I think we have many good reasons to believe this story. Let me list a few.

1) Jesus' life before his death prepared us for his resurrection.

Christianity isn't a story about some random guy who miraculously came back from the dead. It's the story of a man who was a powerful teacher and miracle worker who told us ahead of time that he would be raised from the dead. Throughout the last three years of his life on earth, he gave many powerful teachings which prompted people to wonder how he could have received such wisdom. There's even a story in the Bible about Jesus as a 12-year-old boy who amazed people with his spiritual understanding (see Luke 2:41-47). Not only that, but also Jesus performed many, many miracles. These miracles pointed ahead to Jesus' authority to raise himself from the dead.

Both as a teacher and as a miracle worker, people wondered what kind of person Jesus was. I would like to suggest to you that Jesus' authoritative teaching and his miracles affirm him as the one who has power over death. In fact, Jesus repeatedly predicted both his death and his resurrection. One example is in Mark 8:31, where Jesus said that he "must suffer many things and be rejected by the elders, the chief priests and the teachers of the law, and that he must be killed and after three days rise again." There are many other examples of this. Jesus even predicted specifically how he would die – in Matthew 20:19, he prophesied specific details of his coming death on a cross as well as his resurrection. Also, Jesus prophesied about how he would be "lifted up" (John 3:12 and 12:32) as a prediction of the cross.

We can go even further back and see how the Old Testament predicted Jesus' death and resurrection. Isaiah 53, written about 700 years before Jesus was born, gives specific details about the death of Jesus and then prophesies that he will live again after his death. Psalm 16:9-11 also prophesies about how Jesus would not be abandoned to the grave or see decay, but would take a path of life. It's interesting to note that Jesus *did* go to the grave, but was not *abandoned* there – he was not there long enough to see decay.

So the story of the death and resurrection came from Jesus himself. By all accounts, Jesus was a good man and a powerful teacher. I would like to suggest that he was even more than that. His good deeds, his teachings, and his miracles all were meant to show us that he has power over death.

2) The apostles are credible eyewitnesses.

The transformation that happened in the lives of the apostles is stunning. As I mentioned above, Jesus' disciples were so terrified at the time of his crucifixion that they fled for fear of their lives and one of them even denied three times that he knew Jesus. Shortly after the death of Jesus, his followers were meeting in fear in a locked room.

But then something happened. They saw Jesus, back from the dead. It changed them, powerfully.

If Jesus were still dead, those disciples could have gone back to their previous careers. They might have been embarrassed, but there was no need for them to risk their lives if Jesus were still dead.

Instead, the picture we see is of a group of people convinced that their leader had defeated the power of death. They boldly proclaimed the message of Jesus – and let me remind you, the message of Jesus is what got Jesus crucified in the first place!

Seeing the resurrected Jesus changed everything.

In Acts 1:3, we're told that Jesus interacted with these disciples for a period of 40 days after his death and resurrection. It says he "gave many convincing proofs that he was alive." This was no group hallucination. This was repeated evidence that Jesus was alive again.

But it wasn't just those disciples who told the story of Jesus. As I have mentioned earlier, there were two people who did *not* believe in Jesus until after seeing him in his resurrected form. Both the Apostle James and the Apostle Paul were at first *un*believers. What changed their minds? The resurrection. In the case of the Apostle Paul, he started out persecuting those who believed in Jesus. He wanted to stop this movement, which he, as a Jew, considered to be heretical. You can read his story of how he was convinced of the resurrection in Acts 9:1-30. (Note: he was called "Saul" in that chapter. In Acts 13, he starts being called "Paul.") Almost immediately, he went from persecutor to persecuted – you can read of the first threat on his life in Acts 9:29.

As I mentioned above, these eyewitnesses spread the message of the death and resurrection of Jesus far and wide, and it cost most of them their lives. They were highly motivated to speak of the resurrection of Jesus. Why? The only reasonable answer is because they believed it to be true. Their belief was directly rooted in what they had repeatedly seen with their own eyes and in what Jesus had prophesied repeatedly.

Let me make an important distinction here. Many sincere religious believers, in many different religions, have died for their faith. Many people have gone to the grave, holding onto their beliefs.

But there's something very different in the case of the apostles. They would have known for sure whether the resurrection happened or not.

This isn't like some cult in which the followers sincerely believe that they'll get a ride on a comet. No, the apostles saw the resurrected Jesus. That's what changed their lives.

In *The Case for Christ*, Lee Strobel quotes J.P. Moreland as saying,

> However, the apostles were willing to die for something they had seen with their own eyes and touched with their own hands. They were in a unique position not to just believe Jesus rose from the dead but to know for sure.[12]

What we see from the apostles is credible eyewitness testimony. Nothing in their lives leads us to believe they were chronic liars or were open to mass deception. Instead, it makes more sense to believe that they were sincerely following their risen Lord and Savior. The creed of 1 Corinthians 15:3-8 has stood the test of time as the best explanation – Jesus died for our sins, was buried, was raised on the third day, and appeared to many people, many of whom wrote down their testimony.

This topic of the testimony of the apostles was important for me as a young Christian. As I mentioned before, I wanted to ask hard questions of Christianity, in order to see if there were answers. As such, I began to ask whether we could trust what the apostles wrote about Jesus. Looking into this matter solidified my faith. Instead of being left with questions about the testimony of the apostles, I came away with even deeper conviction that what they wrote was true. I believe the same can happen for you if you will follow where the evidence leads.

3) The tomb really was empty.

In Matthew 28, we get detailed descriptions of what happened on the day Jesus was raised from the dead. We begin to see there the testimony of the first eyewitnesses. Interestingly, Matthew records that the first people to see Jesus were women. That's interesting, because in those days the testimony of women was not considered valid. Surely, Matthew wouldn't have made up this part of the story. Later in the chapter, we read about how Jesus met with his disciples, too.

There's another fascinating part of this story. In the last few verses of Matthew 27, we read that the Jewish leaders remembered what Jesus had said about rising again. Those leaders were concerned that the disciples were going to try to pull off some sort of deception by stealing the body of Jesus, claiming that he was alive. So they were given permission by the Roman leader, Pontius Pilate, to post a guard at the tomb and to seal the tomb. Then, in Matthew 28:11-15, after the guards witnessed an angel opening the tomb, they reported what had occurred. They were told to change their story, saying that the disciples came and stole Jesus' body while the guards were asleep. This is fascinating because, while the Jewish leaders were trying to keep a lid on the resurrection, they admitted something powerful: the tomb was empty. They couldn't stop the spread of Christianity because they couldn't produce the dead body of Jesus. Instead, they made up a story in which we would have to believe that the disciples were liars. As I've shown you above, that is not the case. We know that to be true for at least three reasons. First, the story of the resurrection started with Jesus' very own words. The resurrection wasn't a story invented by the disciples. It came from Jesus. Second, the lives of the disciples show them to be people of very high character. They weren't liars. Their lives were dramatically transformed by seeing Jesus alive again. Third, the dead body of Jesus has never been found. Quite the opposite, there were many eyewitnesses – over 500 of them – who saw him alive again after his death. The story of the disciples stealing the body of Jesus just doesn't hold up. History, once again, is on the side of the resurrection as a real event.

Let me repeat one more point here: the resurrection changed the course of history. Often, new religions fade out when the leader is taken out of the picture. That's what the Romans and Jews tried to do to Jesus and Christianity. But it didn't work. Seeing Jesus alive again after his death emboldened his followers.

4) The resurrection makes sense of the character of God.

This point is more spiritual than historical. I would like to suggest to you that the resurrection of Jesus Christ from the dead is one of the main ways God has revealed himself to us. I believe God chose to do this because the death and resurrection of Jesus teach us about the character of God. Here are a few of the things we learn about God through Jesus' death and resurrection:

First, God is the God of life. In this world, death is a terrible thing. But the resurrection of Jesus reminds us that God has power over death. He doesn't want us to be dead forever. According to what is perhaps the most famous verse in the New Testament, John 3:16, God sent Jesus so that "whoever believes in him shall not perish but have eternal life." The resurrection of Jesus shows us that God has an answer for death. We who believe in him will, like him, inherit eternal life.

Second, God is holy. The word "holy" describes how God is set apart in that he is perfect. He has never sinned and he never will sin. When we sin, we incur punishment from God. Since all of us have sinned, we all deserve punishment. If God didn't intervene, our punishment would lead us to be eternally separated from him, in hell. But, because Jesus willingly offered himself as the perfect sacrifice for our sins, any of us who believe in him will be completely forgiven of all our sins. In that way, our sins were punished at the cross of Jesus Christ.

Third, God is the God of love. As I just mentioned in the paragraph above, the punishment for our sins was placed on Jesus Christ. The reason for that is because God loves us. God saw us in our sinful state and did everything necessary for us to be delivered from it. Jesus, in perfect love for us, willingly offered himself for us. He took your penalty. He died for you. I believe you're reading these words right now because God loves you and wants you to be saved. 1 John 4:9-10 says, "This is how God showed his love among us: He sent his one and only Son into the world that we might live through him. This is love: not that we loved God, but that he loved us and sent his Son as an atoning sacrifice for our sins." The reason we can love God is "because he first loved us" (1 John 4:19).

The fourth book of the New Testament, the Gospel of John (written by the Apostle John), tells the story of the life, death, and resurrection of Jesus. I recommend that you read that book, asking God to reveal himself to you. According to John 1:18, the reason Jesus came was to make God known to us. When we look at who Jesus is and what he has done for us, we learn who God is.

5) The life of Jesus left an impact.

How did the crater get here? At the beginning of this chapter, I started with a hypothetical story in which you were left to wonder how a physical crater came into existence on our planet. Now, I'd like for you to consider again how the resurrection of Jesus has impacted our world.

A man was born in the back country of a nation under the control of a much more powerful empire. Through his authoritative teachings and his powerful miracles, he caused quite a stir, such that both the religious leaders of his nation and the Roman government wanted to put him to death. He was crucified, died, and was buried. But, according to multiple eyewitnesses, he was raised from the dead. Those who saw him alive again spread his story with deep conviction, even to the point of death. Now, billions of people claim to believe in these events.

This crater is so huge that you must give an explanation for why it's here. The theologian C.F.D. Moule wrote of how the resurrection story "rips a great hole in history, a hole the size and shape of Resurrection."[13] As I've shown you in this chapter, the only rational explanation is that Jesus is truly alive again!

6) You can know Jesus.

I'll write more on this in chapter four. For now, I want to show you that you can have a relationship with Jesus. You can walk with him. Yes, it's different than how his disciples walked with him on the earth – we can't see Jesus with our eyes or touch him with our hands. But we can know him. We are invited into a relationship with him in which we will have further proof that he is still alive. In Revelation 3:20, Jesus explains this invitation. He said, "Here I am! I stand at the door and knock. If anyone hears my voice and opens the door, I will come in and eat with that person, and they with me." Those who receive Jesus by faith and who keep walking with him will know him personally and powerfully.

Conclusion

If God exists, he would certainly be able to pull off such a miracle as the resurrection. In chapter one, I showed you that there must be a supernatural explanation for the origin of the universe. God exists. Since God exists, it makes perfect sense that he would reveal himself through the miracle of resurrecting his Son, our Lord Jesus Christ, from the dead. The fact that he did so in plain sight, in real time and on our earth, stands as proof for those who would seek the truth. "He has given proof of this to everyone by raising him from the dead" (Acts 17:31). Think about that. God could have sent Jesus to die for our sins and then brought him immediately to heaven, without anyone seeing the resurrection. But God wanted the resurrection to be a public display, so he allowed lots of people to see the risen Jesus. Many of those people wrote down their testimony and we have it in our hands today. We can know that God raises people from the dead. This means that you, too, can have eternal life – even if your body dies, you can be resurrected and spend eternity with God, if you believe!

To those of you who have hoped that God would give you a sign that he exists, I urge you to see that the God who created the universe, and you, has revealed himself to you through the resurrection of Jesus from the dead.

3. The Bible is the Word of God

"The grass withers and the flowers fall, but the word of our God endures forever."
Isaiah 40:8

In chapter one, I showed you how the fact of the existence of the universe demands that God exists. In chapter two, I showed you which God exists – the one who sent his Son, Jesus Christ our Lord, to die for our sins and to be raised to life again.

In this third chapter, I want to show you what Jesus thinks about the Bible. You'll see that he has a very high opinion of Scripture.

Many people dismiss the Bible as merely the writings of man. On the surface, it's easy to understand why someone would take that view. There are all kinds of religions with all kinds of "sacred" writings. Why not lump the Bible in with the rest of those and simply call them our best attempts to understand the supernatural?

Is there anything different about the Bible? I would give a resounding "yes" to that question, based on the authority of Jesus Christ. As the one who showed his power over death, sent by the one who created the universe, Jesus has the authority to tell us what is true. This authority of Jesus is clearly stated by God the Father in Matthew 17:5, where he said, "This is my Son, whom I love; with him I am well pleased. Listen to him!"

When you want to find the truth of a matter, you want an authority on the subject. Let me use an illustration. If you're sick, you might surf around the internet for a while, trying to figure out what's wrong with you. But if your symptoms persist and you're not quite sure what's wrong with you, you'd probably go to a doctor. Perhaps your family doctor can agree with you that something is indeed wrong, but even he would like to send you to an expert in a specific field of medicine to figure out exactly what is wrong with you. In such cases, we are usually glad to find someone who is an expert in their field, an authority on the matters at hand.

I would like to suggest to you that Jesus Christ is the expert and authority in regard to truth. What I would like to show you in this chapter is that Jesus regarded the Bible, every word of it, to be truth from God. The purpose of this chapter is to advance the conversation: 1) The God who created the universe has revealed himself through what he has created. 2) That same God further revealed himself to us by sending his Son, giving proof of this in the resurrection. 3) That same God has given us a book to teach us who he is and how we should live. If this is all true, we should have the same opinion of the Bible that Jesus does.

What did Jesus believe and say about the Bible?

Because Jesus showed himself to be the Son of God, with his resurrection standing as amazing proof of this, he is in the unique position to tell us about spiritual truth. There are other examples of people being raised from the dead, but Jesus Christ is unique both in that he prophesied that he would rise from the dead (he even gave the specific timeline of three days) and that he said he had the authority to raise up his own life again (see John 10:18). As part of the Trinity, Jesus shows his power over all matters of life and death. As such, we should listen to what he says about spiritual truth.

So what did Jesus believe and say about the Bible? Let's look at a few things. (Note: the word "Bible" is an English word. Jesus used phrases like "Scripture," "the word of God," and "it is written.")

1) Jesus based his life and ministry on the Bible.

Twenty-nine times, the Bible records Jesus as using a word which is translated, "It is written," and that doesn't include the many other times he quoted or referred to Scripture. To Jesus, Scripture was authoritative. Whether he was teaching his disciples or in a disagreement with religious leaders, Jesus regularly quoted the Old Testament, used the phrase "It is written," and assumed that the authority of Scripture would be realized.

Also, Jesus knew that his life would be lived in fulfillment of the Old Testament. Whether in regard to a small detail like his riding a donkey on the way into Jerusalem (see John 12:15, quoting Zechariah 9:9), or in regard to the necessity of his death on the cross in fulfillment of Scripture (see Matthew 26:54), Jesus lived his life according to what the Bible prophesied about him.

Another telling example of how Jesus saw Scripture as authoritative was the time when he was tempted by the devil in the desert. Three times, the devil tempted Jesus to do something. In each case, Jesus refuted the devil with Scripture, using the "It is written" format. Especially telling is what Jesus replied in Matthew 4:4, "Jesus answered, 'It is written: "Man shall not live on bread alone, but on every word that comes from the mouth of God."'" According to Jesus, we are to feast on God's Word.

Also, Jesus claimed that the Old Testament was written about him. In John 5:46, Jesus said, "If you believed Moses, you would believe me, for he wrote about me." After his resurrection, he explained to two of his followers what was said about him in "Moses and all the prophets" and "in all the Scriptures" (see Luke 24:27).

Many other instances could be written about to show this point. Instead, let me summarize with a quote from John Wenham regarding Christ's view of Scripture, "To Him what Scripture said, God said."[1] If that is how Jesus viewed the Bible, why should we view it any lower?

2) Jesus said Scripture cannot be broken.

In a dispute with the religious leaders of his day, Jesus pulled the trump card, quoting Scripture. In the midst of that conversation, Jesus said something very telling about his view of Scripture. In John 10:35, he said, "... and Scripture cannot be set aside." Many translations use the word "broken" instead of "set aside" at the end of that verse. D.A. Carson says this verse means "that the Scripture cannot be annulled or set aside or proved false."[2] The very point Jesus made in this verse was that his opponents in the disagreement should have at least realized the unending authority of Scripture. To Jesus, Scripture was not the opinion of man. Rather, it came with the authority of God and can never be broken.

3) Jesus said his words would never pass away.

So far, I've shown you what Jesus thought of *Old Testament* Scripture. What about the rest of our Bible, the *New Testament*? In Matthew 24:35, we see that Jesus viewed his own words as having the same authority as the rest of Scripture. He said, "Heaven and earth will pass away, but my words will never pass away." Just as Scripture could not be broken or set aside (see point #2 above), so also the words of Jesus would never pass away. Jesus, himself called "the Word" (see John 1:1,14), had the authority to speak such that whatever he said was the Word of God. In this, we are one step closer to seeing that the entire Bible is the Word of God.

4) Jesus promised that the Holy Spirit would reveal God's truth.

The night before Jesus was crucified, he told his followers, "But the Advocate, the Holy Spirit, whom the Father will send in my name, will teach you all things and will remind you of everything I have said to you" (John 14:26). That same evening, Jesus also said of the Holy Spirit, "He will glorify me because it is from me that he will receive what he will make known to you" (John 16:14).

In these two verses, we see the plan of God the Father to send God the Holy Spirit to the followers of Jesus in order to remind them what Jesus said and to make known the things that belong to Jesus. That plan soon came to fruition as the followers of Jesus wrote down what they saw and heard. Every member of the Trinity is involved in the process of the writing of Scripture. It is because of these truths, as well as for other reasons, we believe that God can get his perfect truth to us even through human authors. I'll mention this topic again later, but for now please see that Jesus promised that what would come to us would be from God himself. Again, the Bible is not merely a human book; God is its author.

5) Jesus said that God's Word is truth.

In John 17:17, Jesus prayed to the Father, regarding his followers, "Sanctify them by the truth; your word is truth." To sanctify means to make holy. Jesus prayed that his followers, including us today (as seen in verse 20 of that chapter), would be made holy. For those of us who are already following Jesus, our growth in holiness is one of the most important parts of our lives. Jesus prayed that it would happen "by the truth." Then he added that little comment at the end of the verse, "… your word is truth." Certainly, Jesus didn't say that for the benefit of the Father. God already knows that his Word is truth. No, this was for the benefit of his disciples and, later, for us as we read these words. God's Word is truth.

Please know that Jesus prayed for all of us who would believe in him. He prayed that we would grow in holiness. He wants us to know that this will happen in accordance with the truth of God, and that the Bible is the truth of God. Personally, I am very encouraged to know that the Bible I hold in my hands is not just the words of man. According to Jesus, it is the truth of God and that I can be made holy as I listen to and follow God's

Word. God wants to transform us. Jesus tells us that he does so through his Word.

If the Bible were not the Word of God, Jesus would have had ample opportunity to tell us. If that were the case, he could have said, "Well, you know, Scripture is pretty good. You can learn a lot from it. But you have to be careful with it, because it's really just man's best attempt to understand God." Or, if Jesus had any cautions about taking the Bible as the Word of God, we probably would have a record of the passages he told us not to treat as authoritative. But we don't see anything like that at all in the life of Jesus. Instead, what do we see? We see him treating Scripture as the highest authority, because he believed it to come from God himself.

In summary of these five points about Jesus' view of Scripture, it's interesting that Jesus is called both "the Word" (John 1:1,14) and "the truth" (John 14:6) – because both of those titles are used of Scripture as well. God sent his Son, the Word, to tell us to believe his Word, the Bible. God sent Jesus, the truth, to tell us to believe that the Bible is truth.

What does the rest of the Bible say about the Bible?

Having just shown you that Jesus views the Bible as the Word of God, let's now take a look at what the rest of the Bible says about the Bible. The logic here is this: since Jesus believes the Bible to be the Word of God, we can then trust that the rest of the Bible – even the words not spoken by Jesus – is true. Here are a few examples.

1) Psalm 119:160 says, "All your words are true; all your righteous laws are eternal." This verse is situated in the longest chapter in the Bible, a chapter that reads like a love song for Scripture. It gives an unashamedly high view of the Word of God. Certainly, if this major portion of Scripture were not true, Jesus would have had ample opportunity to tell us so, as I mentioned above. Instead, this verse has stood for about 3,000 years as an example of how we should view the Bible as being eternal truth from God.

2) Isaiah 40:8 says, "The grass withers and the flowers fall, but the word of our God endures forever." This is another verse which mentions the enduring nature of God's Word. It is similar to what Jesus affirmed when he said that Scripture cannot be broken.

3) 2 Timothy 3:16-17 says, "All Scripture is God-breathed and is useful for teaching, rebuking, correcting and training in righteousness, so that the

servant of God may be thoroughly equipped for every good work." This is an important verse because it tells us a little bit about how Scripture came into existence: it is "God-breathed." Although some translations use the word "inspired" instead, that word perhaps isn't strong enough in English to get the point across. It's not that the human authors simply felt that they should write something; it's that the words they wrote were in a very real way breathed by God.

We don't know exactly how the words of human authors were breathed by God. But we do know, from these verses, that the words they wrote came from God. Over the years, many people have suggested how God might have done this. The consensus is that God was able to guide the process of the writings such that both the individual character traits of the author and the authority of the Word of God are combined in what was written. When the Apostle Paul wrote, he used language unique to himself – his writings sound different than those of the Apostle John, for example. Yet both Paul's words and John's words in the Bible can be said to be the Word of God, because he breathed them.

Let me say one other thing about these verses. They follow a verse (2 Timothy 3:15) which tells us that Scripture is able to make a person wise for salvation through faith in Christ Jesus. Although this gets into the topic of my next chapter, let me say now that God gave us his Word so that we could be saved from death and into eternal life. It is of utmost importance that we listen to God's Word!

4) 2 Peter 1:21 says, "For prophecy never had its origin in the human will, but prophets, though human, spoke from God as they were carried along by the Holy Spirit." The phrase "carried along" is an interesting one in this verse. It's the same word as is used twice in Acts 27:15-17 to speak of how a ship is driven along by wind. For the purposes of this verse in 2 Peter, what we see is that prophets did not make up their own direction, but rather were empowered by God to say what they said. This verse also highlights the role of the Holy Spirit in this process, which again is exactly what Jesus mentioned the night before he was crucified in John 14:26 and 16:14.

5) In their writings, some of the New Testament authors testify that they wrote what they saw and heard. For examples, see John 20:30, 21:24; 2 Peter 3:16-18; 1 John 1:1-3; and Revelation 1:9-11. Two other books, both written by the historian Luke (who should rightly be recognized as one of

the great historians of his time) begin with his account of how he gathered his material from eyewitnesses – see Luke 1:1-4 and Acts 1:1-3. In this, the New Testament is vastly different than so many other religious writings. It claims to come directly from those who literally walked with Jesus.

6) Two New Testament authors claim the term "Scripture" for the New Testament. In 2 Peter 3:16, Peter speaks of Paul's letters, comparing them with "the other Scriptures." Grammatically, this puts Paul's letters in the same category of Scripture as the Old Testament. As such, it deserves to be viewed as the kind of Scripture Jesus told us cannot be broken. Also, in 1 Timothy 5:18, the Apostle Paul quoted Luke 10:7 in the same verse in which he quoted an Old Testament verse. Paul called both of them "Scripture."

7) When Paul preached to the people of the city of Thessalonica, he applauded them for receiving his message "not as a human word, but as it actually is, the word of God" (1 Thessalonians 2:13).

According both to Jesus and to the rest of Scripture, the Bible is the Word of God. Yet some people would still bring up an objection that the words of the Bible have been tainted over time. According to this argument, it's possible that the words of the Bible were originally perfect, but now – through years of copying and translation – they are not.

Is the Bible you hold in your hands today the Word of God?

Other authors have presented a much more thorough explanation of this question than I intend to do here. For reference, I highly recommend chapter three of Lee Strobel's *The Case for Christ,* in which he interviews Dr. Bruce Metzger. Additionally, you could read chapter four of *More Than a Carpenter* by Josh McDowell.

For the purposes of this book, I am glad to tell you two things: 1) Jesus himself validated the Old Testament. 2) The New Testament stands head and shoulders above any other historical writing of its time period. Allow me to expand briefly on these two points.

As I've mentioned above (so I won't belabor the point here!), Jesus validated the Old Testament. By the time Jesus came to earth, the Old Testament had been widely circulated and read in cities all over the Roman Empire. If there were any problems with the Old Testament, Jesus could have corrected them. Again, he did nothing of the sort. He did the opposite – he validated the Old Testament as the Word of God.

But what about the New Testament? As I just mentioned, the validity of the New Testament, when compared with any other historical writing of its time, is unmatched. Part of the reason for this is the efforts God's people went to in order to copy these writings. Treating them as Holy Scripture, Christians faithfully copied and circulated the writings of the New Testament to the point that there are *far* more copies of the New Testament than any other historical writing of the time period.

Along these lines, we can picture a book of the New Testament being written. Then, in order to circulate that book to other churches in other cities, the book was copied. Then, from those locations, the books were copied again. What we can do today is compare a copy sent in one direction to a copy sent in another direction, because we have existing copies from multiple locations. Sometimes, yes, there are mistakes in copying. (By the way, I would never suggest that every copy of the Bible is accurate, merely the original.) But we can compare those mistakes and come to a very high degree of certainty regarding what was in the original. Looking into these copies, even with the mistakes the copyists made, will show you that we have a very reliable record of what was first written. Using this evidence from the copies (called *manuscripts*), we can rest assured that we have the exact wording of over 99 percent of the New Testament. Wayne Grudem says of this percentage that "they are exact copies of the originals."[3]

Therefore, it won't work to say that we used to have the Bible, but now we have something less than the Word of God. Historically, the evidence shows us that we have reliable copies. Personally, you can hear from God as you read his Word, in your language.

What do theologians say about the Bible today?
Of course, one could find a theologian to say just about anything. But on this topic of the authority of the Bible as God's Word, there is a high degree of unity among many theologians. In this section, I want to give you some rapid-fire statements from some leading theologians about the authority and truthfulness of the Bible.

- Paul Feinberg: "The Scriptures are God's speech."[4] "It is the concept of a *wholly true* Bible for which I contend."[5]

- John Wenham: "The writings are authoritative, not because of the human author, but because God is regarded as the ultimate author."[6]
- Al Mohler: "When the Bible speaks, God speaks"[7] "The Bible consistently and relentlessly claims to be nothing less than the perfect Word of the perfect God who breathed its very words."[8] "God wrote a book."[9]
- Kevin Vanhoozer: *"God's authoritative Word is wholly true and trustworthy in everything it claims about what was, what is, and what will be."*[10] (Italics are original.)
- Wayne Grudem: "All the words in Scripture are God's words."[11]
- D.A. Carson: "… and we who are Christians insist that God has disclosed himself supremely in the pages of these documents."[12]

One other important way to verify the truthfulness of the Bible

As I've mentioned before, many religions claim to have authoritative truth. Some of them will ask you to read their holy writings and ask if God is speaking to you, perhaps in some sort of burning inside of you. Is that how truth works? Should we expect ourselves to be able to verify truth simply by our perception of what is written? I would answer both yes and no to that question.

On the one hand, I would like to remind you where I started this discussion: with the Creator God who revealed himself in his creation and with his Son, Jesus Christ our Lord, who was raised from the dead. From there, I built a case for the truthfulness of the Bible that comes directly from what Jesus said, and then also from what the rest of Scripture says about itself. In that sense, my case for the authority of Scripture rests on facts that are outside of myself. I would hope that no one would merely "trust their gut" if the evidence shows a religion's writings to be false. In the case of Christianity, the evidence points to Scripture being true.

On the other hand, having already shown outside facts, I would like to suggest to you that we can recognize the truthfulness of the Christian Bible as we read it. As we dig into what God has given us, we can hear directly from him. For about 25 years, I have been reading the Bible regularly. I have found it to be what it says it is, the "living and active" Word of God (see Hebrews 4:12). I have seen God sanctify me, just as Jesus prayed in John 17:17.

I believe that you, too, can see the power of God's Word at work in your life. I urge you to give it a try. One of the best pieces of advice I have on this topic is that you would start with the Gospel of John, the fourth book in the New Testament. It is 21 chapters long – perhaps you start by reading one chapter per day. I would recommend that you read it slowly enough so that you can understand what you're reading. As you're reading, talk to God. Ask him to reveal himself to you. Maybe you could start out by saying, "God, if you're out there, I'd like to know you. If you wrote this book, I'll listen."

What kind of power should we expect in the Word of God?

If the Bible really is the Word of God, what should we expect it to do in our lives? As I just mentioned, I think we should expect life change.

To highlight this point, I would like to remind you how God created the universe. In chapter one, I told you that God is the creator. But do you know *how* he created? In Genesis 1, the repeated phrase is, "And God said…" (Gen. 1:3,6,9,14,20,24). Psalm 33:6 says, "By the word of the LORD the heavens were made, their starry host by the breath of his mouth." Hebrews 11:3 says, "By faith we understand that the universe was formed at God's command."

God's Word is so powerful that it created our universe. Imagine what it can do in your life.

An encouragement and a warning

God's Word is a powerful force in our world. As such, it should be treated properly. For those who will humbly listen to God, I have some encouraging words. For those who will not, there is something you need to hear now, before it's too late.

The encouragement for those who will listen to God is that God wants to speak to you. All throughout the Bible, we see evidence of God speaking to his people. When he first created Adam and Eve, he spoke to them. He then spoke to Abraham, giving him great and wonderful promises. He then spoke to his people through Moses, telling his people how they could live in a relationship with God. God continued to speak through prophets. Then, in an amazing turn of events, God sent his Son, Jesus Christ, who spoke many words to us – words about God, words about life, words that define who we are better than we could define ourselves.

If you will set your heart to hear from God, he will speak to you. When we approach the Bible, we should have the attitude of the young boy, Samuel, who said, "Speak, for your servant is listening" (1 Samuel 3:10b). An attitude of humility will go a long way. Isaiah 66:2b says, "These are the ones I look on with favor: those who are humble and contrite in spirit, and who tremble at my word."

However, for those who will not listen to God's Word, Jesus had something to say. In John 12:48, he said, "There is a judge for the one who rejects me and does not accept my words; the very words I have spoken will condemn them at the last day." I don't mention this because I take any pleasure in thinking about people receiving judgment – I would much rather you receive blessing from God! I mention this because Jesus had a lot to say about judgment. It is not accurate to paint Jesus as merely a kind, soft spirit who would never offend anyone. He offended lots of people when they were in error. And he had a lot to say about eternal judgment. Why? He warns us not to be on the wrong side of this. We will be on the right side of this if we accept his words.

We do not stand in judgment over God's Word. Yes, we should look carefully into this matter, to see whether the Bible is God's Word. But my conclusion on this matter is that we were created by God's Word and we will be judged according to his Word.

You are what you eat

You've probably heard the phrase, "You are what you eat." In one sense, it's literally true. Many of the nutrients and fats you eat become part of your body or the energy your body uses to function. That's why healthy eating is linked to overall health.

Do you remember the analogy Jesus used about the Word of God being like food? In Matthew 4:4, he said, "Man shall not live on bread alone, but on every word that comes from the mouth of God." Jesus implied that we are to feast on God's Word. Spiritually speaking, it sustains us.

Let's follow this analogy. After you eat a meal, how long is it until you get hungry again? For me, after about two hours, I start to think about a snack or my next meal – sometimes sooner! My body keeps urging me to eat. Without regular intake of food, we wouldn't survive. God made our bodies to need food in this way.

In his wisdom, I think God made our bodies like this, in part, as an analogy of how our souls were made to feast continually on his Word. Practically speaking, I make it my aim to meet with God in his Word every day. Ideally, there would also be other parts of my day in which I interact with God's Word at various levels.

There are many messages in this world which attempt to get you to live a certain way. Think about commercials as one example. Multiple times a day, we are bombarded with messages that we should purchase certain products. The creators of those
commercials are trying to change your life through their message.

Since we live in a world with so many messages, we should frequently humble ourselves before God and listen to his message, his Word, the Bible.

The Bible as a blueprint

At the risk of injecting too many illustrations, allow me to use another one to close out this chapter. One summer, I worked on a construction crew. For most of the days, I worked on the building we were constructing. Honestly, I didn't have too much of a clue of what I should be doing. I kept hoping people would tell me what to do. But occasionally, I got a glimpse behind the scenes. During some of my lunch breaks, I was invited into the trailer in which the blueprints for the job were located. While there, I would see the foreman and other leaders of the crew analyzing the blueprints. When lunch was over, I would see how the crew was directed to work in line with the blueprints. Although I wasn't in charge of the project (thankfully!), I saw the importance of the blueprints. Everything we did as a crew was meant to line up with the blueprints. As such, I started to notice how regularly the foreman went to study the blueprints.

There should be a similar pattern for us. We don't always know what to do in life. Yes, we have some ideas of what we'd like to do and we can figure out some of the things we're supposed to do. But how can we have any confidence that what we're actually doing is what we're supposed to do? That's where the blueprints come in to play. God has given us a book, kind of like construction blueprints. The Bible tells us how to live.

When I first started to read the Bible, I expected to learn about God. I also expected to learn about how to live. What surprised me was how much I learned about who I am. You see, the Bible doesn't just tell us what to do. It also explains our life. I would like to suggest to you that the best pattern of life is one in which you continually examine the blueprints, the Bible.

The same God who created the universe by his Word continues to speak his Word to us through the written words of the Bible. God gave us a book. Let us be people who listen.

4. Jesus Christ is Savior and Lord

"Now this is eternal life: that they know you, the only true God, and Jesus Christ, whom you have sent."
John 17:3

"If you declare with your mouth, 'Jesus is Lord,' and believe in your heart that God raised him from the dead, you will be saved."
Romans 10:9

In the first three chapters of this book, I have told you things that are true about God: 1) God is the creator of the universe. 2) Jesus was raised from the dead. 3) The Bible is the Word of God.

But I want to do something that I believe is more important in this chapter. I want to do more than tell you about God. I want you to know God.

Let me use an analogy. You can know a lot about a person without knowing them. Think of a famous person – perhaps a famous athlete, an actress, a president, or a monarch. You can watch them on TV or the movies. You can follow them on Twitter. You can learn things about their lives on the internet. You can get to know a lot of things about them. But you can do all those things without actually knowing them. In that sense, if you actually had the opportunity to meet them – or much more, to become their friend – then not only would you know about that person, he or she would know you and vice versa.

God doesn't want us simply to know things about him. He wants us to know him, to live in a relationship with him that will last for the rest of eternity.

What I want to do in this chapter is to tell you what the Bible says about how we can know God. It has everything to do with the one God sent, Jesus Christ. I would like to tell you who Jesus Christ is by explaining two of the important names for him in the New Testament: Savior and Lord. The goal of this chapter is that you would see not only the things that are true about God (like the things I mentioned in chapters 1-3), but also that you would have a relationship with God through faith in Jesus Christ. Here's another way of saying this: because of the things God has revealed to us, we should realize that God desires to be with us as we respond rightly to him by faith.

The fact that God created you, sent his Son to die for you, and gave you his Word should cause you to see that you were created for a relationship with God. According to Scripture, which Jesus said cannot be broken, this relationship has to do with believing in Jesus.

Over 16 years of full-time ministry, my preferred way of explaining this to people has to do with those two names for Jesus that I've already mentioned: Savior and Lord. Let's take a look at what each of those names mean and how we should respond.

Jesus Christ is Savior

This title for Jesus is incredibly easy to understand. The fact that he is called "Savior" simply means that he saves us. Jesus told us that's what he came to do. In Luke 19:10, he said, "For the Son of Man came to seek and to save the lost." 1 Timothy 1:15b says, "Christ Jesus came into the world to save sinners."

To be saved, in everyday language, means to be rescued from something. We could talk about a person being saved from a burning building or saving a cat from a tree. We even talk about saving money. Obviously, the context of the word "saved" varies from situation to situation. In regard to Jesus, it's important to recognize what he saves us from.

So what do we need to be saved from? Over the years, I've asked this question to lots of people, and they usually come up with a pretty good answer – I've heard people say that we need to be saved from sin, death, hell, and even from ourselves. Each of those answers highlight something important about us: we have all done things that deserve punishment. In order to agree with that last statement, you should understand both what we have done wrong (that's what the Bible calls sin) and the punishment we deserve for our sin.

Our sinfulness is clearly stated in Romans 3:23, which says, "For all have sinned and fall short of the glory of God." The standard is the glory of the God who is perfect in all his ways. He has never sinned, nor will he ever sin. That's a high standard. Unfortunately, a lot of people assume there is a different standard. A lot of people I've talked to assume that the standard is simply that we would try our best, or that we would be compared with the people around us. People say things like, "I think God will see that I've tried to be a good person," or, "I haven't done anything really bad, like murder." If that were the standard, then a lot of people would get into heaven for doing good things. But that's not what the Bible says. In fact, James 2:10 tells us that, even if we only stumbled at one point, we'd be guilty of breaking the entire law. When a person gets punished in a court of law, they don't get judged by the good things they have done; they get judged according to what they have done wrong. Following that pattern, none of us could say that we have never done anything wrong. We have all sinned; we have all fallen short of the glory of God.

Then, like I said, we should understand the punishment for our sin. Romans 6:23a says, "For the wages of sin is death." The word "wages" in that verse is a word that could be used for your paycheck – if you do the work, you get a paycheck; you earned the money by what you did at your job. Similarly, we had all earned a death penalty by what we had done wrong. That death penalty would be not only a physical death (like the kind of death that came into the world when Adam and Eve sinned, the kind of death we face as we grow old or face sickness or catastrophe), but also a spiritual death in the fires of hell.

Now let me stop here for a moment, because I've just told you something to which lot of people object. Many people wonder why the punishment for our sin is so severe. Someone might say, "If God is a God of love, why would he send anyone to hell?" It's a great question, one that we shouldn't be afraid to ask, but also one for which we should seek to find an answer. The answer has to do, again, with the perfection of God. He is perfect; he never does anything wrong. But we sin. We might want to brush our sins under the rug and say, "They're not so bad!" But they are bad. You see, every sin we commit is an act of rebellion against the God who loves us. God has good plans for us. He wants what's best for us. When we sin, we choose a different path, one of our own making. We, by our sin, had shown a willingness to reject God's path. In that sense we, like Adam and Eve, rejected life and chose death.

We need a proper understanding of our sin. It is no small deal. I think the best way to understand our sin is to look at the payment required to take care of our sin problem. Here, again, we might have a much different idea about our sin than God does. Like I said before, we might simply think we could brush our sins under the rug and pretend they never happened. Or we might think it best if God simply overlooked our sinful mistakes and let us into heaven anyway. But that's not God's view of sin. In God's way of dealing with our sin, we see that it is such a problem that the only solution was for him to send his beloved Son, Jesus Christ, to die for us. Jesus didn't die for our sins because they weren't all that bad; he died for our sins because they *are* all that bad! We might think sin is just an unfortunate mistake. In reality, our sin results in death. Ephesians 2:1 says, "As for you, you were dead in your transgressions and sins."

Because we sinned, there needed to be payment of death. We had earned it. Those were our wages. If left to ourselves, that would mean eternal separation from God, in hell. But in his mercy, God sent Jesus to die for us. That's what it means for him to be our Savior.

As our Savior, Jesus took our sin penalty upon himself. Have you ever wondered why Jesus was sent to earth as a human being? Think about it. The penalty for our sin was human death. Jesus, as a perfect human being, was able to offer himself for our sins, as a substitute in our place. As a perfect person, he had no sin of his own that needed to be punished. Therefore, he could offer himself in our place – because he came as a human, his death could be offered in place of ours. Our sin was paid for when Jesus died on the cross! This happened because God loves us. Romans 5:8 says, "But God demonstrates his own love for us in this: While we were still sinners, Christ died for us."

This is the solution! Through the cross of Jesus Christ, God shows himself to be both the holy God and the God of love. He is holy in that our sin was punished – it was punished in the body of Jesus Christ. But God is also the God of love in that he offers forgiveness through Jesus. This is why F.F. Bruce calls the cross "the climax of divine revelation."[1] When we look at the cross, we learn beautiful things about God.

But to whom is this forgiveness offered? Who did Jesus save when he died on the cross for our sins? The Bible clearly tells us that this forgiveness is for all who receive Jesus, for those who believe in him. Perhaps the most famous verse in the New Testament is John 3:16, which says, "For God so loved the world that he gave his one and only Son, that whoever believes in him shall not perish but have eternal life." Along those same lines, John 1:12 says about our response to Jesus, "Yet to all who did receive him, to those who believed in his name, he gave the right to become children of God."

Jesus died on the cross to save us from our sins, to save us from the eternal fire of hell. As shown by his resurrection, we see that he saves us into eternal life. If we are saved by Jesus, we are saved forever. This happened not because we deserved it, but because God loves us. That's an amazing truth – God loves us so much that he does not want us to perish, but to have eternal life. "But because of his great love for us, God, who is rich in mercy, made us alive with Christ even when we were dead in transgressions – it is by grace you have been saved" (Ephesians 2:4-5).

We can and should be very thankful that God sent Jesus to be our Savior. If we rightly understood the magnitude of our sin problem, every one of us would want a Savior. Although some people might make up an imaginary hell, full of non-stop partying with sinners, there is no true life apart from God. Jesus himself described hell as a place of "eternal punishment" (Matthew 25:46), as well as a place of "weeping and gnashing of teeth" (Matthew 25:30). I urge you not to be on a course set for hell!

So please, receive Jesus Christ as your Savior!

But as I mentioned earlier, there is one other name for Jesus that we must consider. If we are to receive Jesus, it is important to recognize that he is not only Savior, but also Lord.

Jesus Christ is Lord

I hope that what you are about to read will help you understand more fully who Jesus Christ is. It has been clearly revealed to us in the Bible. Yet I feel that this teaching about Jesus Christ as Lord has been widely under-appreciated.

So let me start this section by asking you a question: What do you think it means that Jesus Christ is Lord?

Without question, the New Testament claims that Jesus Christ is Lord – that title is used of him many, many times. According to Romans 10:9, those who confess that Jesus is Lord and who believe in his resurrection will be saved. According to Philippians 2:11, it will one day be a universally acknowledged truth that Jesus Christ is Lord.

But what does it mean that Jesus Christ is Lord?

I would like to share with you two answers to that question. Both are correct – they each show us something about who Jesus is. The first answer doesn't usually come as a surprise to most people – people with even a basic understanding of the Bible usually are aware of it. But the second answer is one that I have found far too many people do not know.

1) The name "Lord" is the name for God.

If you're reading your Old Testament and you see the name "Lord" (some translations helpfully put it in all capital letters – "LORD"), you are right to assume that it usually refers to God the Father. In Christianity, we often refer to God the Father as the first member of the Trinity.

But something shocking happens in the New Testament. That name "Lord," used for God the Father, is shared with Jesus Christ. This is shocking, because in the Old Testament, God says, "I am the LORD, and there is no other" (Isaiah 45:18d). The name "Lord" is no ordinary name. It is the divine, personal name of God.

Let me show you some ways in which this name "Lord" is shared with Jesus in the New Testament.

- In John 20:28, as the Apostle Thomas first laid his eyes on the resurrected Jesus, he said to him, "My Lord and my God!" Interestingly, Jesus did nothing to correct him. (In fact, this is right along the lines of one of the best reasons to believe that Jesus is part of the Trinity – he accepts the worship which is only rightly accepted by God. Many other verses in the New Testament show this same pattern.)
- In Acts 2, the Apostle Peter gave a sermon to a large crowd of people several weeks after Jesus' resurrection. In that sermon, he quoted three Old Testament passages which refer to the Lord. Again, we are right to assume those passages speak of God the Father. But then, right after Peter quoted the third passage, he said, "Therefore let all Israel be assured of this: God has made this Jesus, whom you crucified, both Lord and Messiah" (Acts 2:36). To Peter, both the Father and the Son can be called "Lord."
- Similarly, the Apostle Paul says in Romans 10:13, quoting the Old Testament, "Everyone who calls on the name of the Lord will be saved." But a few verses earlier, he urged people to confess that "Jesus is Lord" (Romans 10:9).
- In Philippians 2:6-11, Paul tells us how Jesus came to earth as a human and as a servant. He goes on to speak about the death of Jesus – it looked as if Jesus had gone lower and lower. But then, in verse 9, we read about how God exalted Jesus and "gave him the name that is above every name." In the

55

following two verses, we see how every knee will bow before Jesus and how every tongue will "acknowledge that Jesus Christ is Lord, to the glory of God the Father." This is notable because Paul is drawing from language in the Old Testament, specifically from Isaiah 45, in which God says, "for I am God, and there is no other" (verse 22). In the following verse, we read how God has sworn by himself that every knee will bow before him and every tongue will swear allegiance. In verses 21 and 24 of that chapter, we see the name "LORD" used of God the Father.

Why do I mention all of this? Because I want you to see that Jesus Christ shares the name "Lord" with God the Father. When we believe in Jesus, we don't merely agree to some truths about a man who lived 2,000 years ago; we embrace the truth of the Lord. When we receive Jesus Christ, we enter into a relationship with God.

Like I said, this is one of two things meant by the name "Lord." Let's move to the second.

2) The title "Lord" means "Master."

When the Old Testament Hebrew name "LORD" is quoted in the New Testament, the authors picked a new word. That's not what they usually did with names. For example, when they spoke of Moses, they used Greek letters to make a name that sounded like the Hebrew for Moses. They didn't pick a new word which had the same meaning as "Moses." They made a name that sounded like "Moses" in Greek. This would be the same as if you went to a foreign country in which your name wasn't a common name. You might probably still use your name and ask people to learn how to say it. They might change it a little – like my teacher in China who tried to get my name right, but ended up calling me "Erocco."

But like I just said, this isn't what the New Testament authors did with the name "LORD." Instead, they chose to use an existing Greek word in place of the name "LORD." The word they chose was *kurios*. This word has a range of meaning from "sir" or "owner" all the way up to the divine name "LORD." Included in this range of meanings is a word that means "Master." As always in the Bible, context will usually tell us which meaning is meant. Many, many times, the plain meaning of the word *kurios* is the Old Testament name "LORD." But in some other places, we learn something rich about the title "Lord" – we learn that it carries the

56

meaning of "Master." When we understand this truth, we will understand in greater detail what it means to know Jesus as Lord.

So what does it mean that Jesus is Master?

Let's start out with a verse found on the lips of Jesus himself. In Luke 6:46, Jesus said, "Why do you call me, 'Lord, Lord,' and do not do what I say?" Do you see what Jesus expects of his followers in that verse? He expects that they would not only hear him, but also obey him. In the following verses, Jesus told a famous story of two people who built houses. One laid his foundation on a rock while the other "built a house on the ground without a foundation" (verse 49). The outcomes were drastically different – the house on the rock was not shaken, while the foundation-less house was completely destroyed. What was the difference? Jesus told this story to contrast two people, both of whom heard the words of Jesus, but only one of whom "put them into practice."

To know Jesus as Master, it is not enough simply to hear him. As Master, Jesus expects that we would listen, obey, and put into practice what he says.

Let me use a parable, now, to drive home this point. In Mark 12:1-11, Jesus told a story about a man who hired some people to work in his vineyard. Here is the parable:

> [1] Jesus then began to speak to them in parables: "A man planted a vineyard. He put a wall around it, dug a pit for the winepress and built a watchtower. Then he rented the vineyard to some farmers and moved to another place. [2] At harvest time he sent a servant to the tenants to collect from them some of the fruit of the vineyard. [3] But they seized him, beat him and sent him away empty-handed. [4] Then he sent another servant to them; they struck this man on the head and treated him shamefully. [5] He sent still another, and that one they killed. He sent many others; some of them they beat, others they killed.
> [6] "He had one left to send, a son, whom he loved. He sent him last of all, saying, 'They will respect my son.'
> [7] "But the tenants said to one another, 'This is the heir. Come, let's kill him, and the inheritance will be ours.' [8] So they took him and killed him, and threw him out of the vineyard.

9 "What then will the owner of the vineyard do? He will come and kill those tenants and give the vineyard to others. 10 Haven't you read this passage of Scripture: 'The stone the builders rejected has become the cornerstone; 11 the Lord has done this, and it is marvelous in our eyes'?"

Interestingly, in this parable, when we first met him, the one who owned the vineyard is simply called "a man." He hired people to work for him. When he sent servants to collect his share of the fruit, the hired workers (tenants) mistreated and even killed the servants. If you were first reading this story, when you hear that the man thought to send his son, you might think to yourself, "No, don't do it! Don't you see how they treated the others you sent!" But the man sent his son anyway.

By this point in the story, it's probably clear to you that the man who owned the vineyard refers to God and the son is God's Son, Jesus Christ. Just like Jesus was killed by those to whom he was sent, so also the son in this parable was killed. But why?

You see, the people in this parable started to think they had the right to run that vineyard the way they wanted to. In this parable, the owner of the vineyard was away. In our daily life, it can feel very much like God is distant. If we feel that way, it's all too easy for us to come up with our own ideas of how to live. If we're set on living according to our own ways, the thought of someone else telling us how to live can be very unappealing.

But in order to run the vineyard the way they wanted to, the hired workers needed to get rid of the son. You see, if the son is still around, he carries the authority of the owner. So the plan of the hired workers was to kill the son. Then, they thought, they could run the vineyard as they pleased.

Did their plan work? Of course not! Killing the son only drew the wrath of the owner. Here's an important point in this parable: when we first met him, the one who owned the vineyard was simply called "a man" in verse 1. But when we read about him again in verse 9, as the one who clearly has authority over the workers and the vineyard, he is given a new title – in Greek, it's *kurios*. It's often translated as "owner," but it clearly carries the meaning of "Master" here. He is not just some man who happens to own a vineyard. He is the one who has complete authority – both over the vineyard and over the workers he has put there to work in it.

In response to the workers' rejection of his son, the Master of the vineyard killed the tenants. But then also note that it says he will "give the vineyard to others" (verse 10). Both points are important – let me expand on them.

First, to those who reject the Son, God will send punishment. It is of eternal significance how we respond to Jesus. Ultimately, there are only two choices: either we receive him or we reject him. Either we give our lives to Jesus or we put ourselves in with the people who killed him. Although it might feel to us that there's a middle option, there will be no middle option on judgment day. Either we are with Jesus or against him. Earlier, I mentioned the severity of the punishment for rejecting Jesus. This parable highlights how important it is for us to be with Jesus, not against him.

Let's stop here for a moment. Who would really do such a thing? Who would kill the son of the Master? In parable form, it's hard to believe that anyone would actually kill their boss' son. What we need to do is to figure out what this parable refers to in real life. At first, the vineyard referred to Israel and the tenants were the spiritual leaders of Israel, the ones who sent Jesus to his death. But in verse 9, Jesus explained that he was looking to give the vineyard to others. We should strive to be those others to whom the vineyard is given. For us, then, the vineyard includes everything we do – it's the place where God expects us to bear fruit for him. Bearing fruit in the Bible often has the meaning of pleasing God by living according to his ways. Many people don't live like that. If the vineyard corresponds to our experience on earth, far too many people live here according to their own ways, not God's ways. You see, they live as if the Master has gone away. They pretend to have the authority to direct their own path of life. If the Son were to come and say otherwise, they might very well reject him. Although they might not physically put anyone to death, denying Jesus has a worse spiritual consequence than murder.

So let me ask you a very pointed question: are you honoring God by living according to his ways, following what his Son, Jesus Christ, has told you? Or do you live for yourself? It's awfully tempting for us in this vineyard to live for ourselves. But rebelling against the authority of the Master has consequences. That leads to the next point.

Second, as I have already mentioned, God is looking to give the vineyard to others. As the Master of the vineyard, God wants people here who will do his work. Again, the vineyard for us represents all that we do to serve God. God wants us to work here as if we were working for him.

The things you do in your everyday life are things you can do as if you were directly serving God. In the vineyard, every bit of work done to produce a crop was supposed to be done ultimately for the Master, according to his wishes. It's the exact same for us in daily life. In a section of the Bible which tells servants how to obey their masters, Colossians 3:23 says, "Whatever you do, work
at it with all your heart, as working for the Lord, not for human masters." Similarly, Colossians 3:17 says, "And whatever you do,
whether in word or deed, do it all in the name of the Lord Jesus, giving thanks to God the Father through him." How much of your life does this encompass? Everything! Whatever you do!

Every moment of our lives is a moment that should be lived according to the truth that we have a heavenly Master. We can bring honor and glory to God by serving him. We would bring dishonor to him by rejecting his ways.

(Note: in this parable of the vineyard, the Master refers to God the Father. However, as I've already shown you, the title "Master" can refer either to the Father or the Son in the New Testament. This parable teaches what the word "Master" means and we can apply it to our relationship with Jesus as Lord.)

We must receive Jesus Christ as Savior and Lord

I have laid out in this chapter that Jesus Christ is Savior and Lord. The crux of the issue is this: have you received Jesus as Savior and Lord? Romans 10:9 says, "If you declare with your mouth, 'Jesus is Lord,' and believe in your heart that God raised him from the dead, you will be saved."

To receive Jesus as Savior means you must recognize that you have sinned against God and that you need Jesus to save you. There is no other way for your sins to be forgiven. Jesus said, "I am the way and the truth and the life. No one comes to the Father except through me" (John 14:6). Acts 4:12 says of Jesus, "Salvation is found in no one else, for there is no other name under heaven given to mankind by which we must be saved." Please know that God loves you and is pleased to forgive those who receive Jesus by faith. God already knows you have sinned – don't try to hide it.

Also, to receive Jesus is to receive him as Lord. When we receive Jesus, we do not only ask him to forgive our sins and give us eternal life. We also are to give our lives to him, to submit to him as our Master.

At this point, I would like to remind you that there are only two paths. Although God grants us time to seek, we must each either receive or reject Jesus. We must not pretend to accept the salvation he gives as Savior without submitting to him as our Master. Jesus is Lord; we are to receive him as such.

Let me introduce one more Bible word that should help clear this up: repentance. When Jesus started his public ministry on earth, he said, "The kingdom of God has come near. Repent and believe the good news!" (Mark 1:15).

To repent means to turn away from sin, both in our thoughts and in our actions. On our own, we had all shown ourselves to be sinners, choosing a path of our own liking. To repent is to admit that we have sinned against God, to ask for forgiveness, and to ask God to give us the strength to walk on the path he has for us.

So I urge you to believe in Jesus, receiving him as Savior and Lord.

A personal story

When I was in high school, I remember hearing this message about Jesus for the first time. I heard that my sins needed to be forgiven. I was told that I should ask Jesus into my heart. I remember a preacher quoting Revelation 3:20, in which Jesus says, "Here I am! I stand at the door and knock. If anyone hears my voice and opens the door, I will come in and eat with that person, and they with me." That verse describes a new relationship with God. That relationship begins when we ask Jesus to come in. In that verse, the door can represent your heart or your life. As I heard that message, several thoughts went through my mind. Here are a few of them.

- I knew I had sinned. Growing up in church, I had heard lots of things that I should and shouldn't be doing, and I knew I wasn't perfect. Some people perhaps think they have done nothing for which forgiveness is necessary. Not me. I knew I had fallen short of God's perfect standard.
- I wondered why I hadn't heard this message before. Maybe I wasn't listening in church. Maybe the church I went to didn't talk about receiving Jesus. Maybe my heart wasn't ready. But that message, if true, would change everything. So I decided to look into the Bible to see if this preacher was right. It turns out he was. The Bible has lots to say about receiving Jesus.

61

- As eager as I was to have my sins forgiven, I was also scared about what God would do if I gave my life to him. I knew that to receive Jesus was to give control to him. If I would receive him as Master, then I could no longer pretend to be the master of my own life. I was scared that God would make me be a missionary to Africa!
- Although I knew God was speaking directly to my heart, I was scared what my friends would think if I asked Jesus to be my Savior and Lord. I thought they might think less of me.

After a brief time (maybe a week?) of looking into the Bible to make sure that message was accurate, I knew that I should ask Jesus to be my Savior and Lord. Even though I still was concerned about what that might mean for my future, I deeply sensed God's love for me and I couldn't stand the thought of living my life apart from God's plan anymore. So I prayed to receive Jesus as my Savior and Lord.

Will you receive Jesus as Savior and Lord?

Again, there are two options: receive or reject Jesus. John 3:36 says, "Whoever believes in the Son has eternal life, but whoever rejects the Son will not see life, for God's wrath remains on them."

To receive Jesus, like I said before, is to acknowledge your need to have your sins forgiven and to ask Jesus to be your Lord and Master.

To receive Jesus, you could pray a prayer like this: God, thank you for your love for me. Thank you for sending Jesus to die for my sins and to rise again from the dead. I acknowledge that I have sinned. I pray to receive Jesus as my Savior. Please forgive me for all of my sins. I pray also to receive Jesus as Lord. I give my life to you, God. Help me to live the life you want me to live. Amen.

We can have great assurance that God will hear and answer that kind of prayer. Listen to what 1 John 5:11-15 says,

> [11] And this is the testimony: God has given us eternal life, and this life is in his Son.
> [12] Whoever has the Son has life; whoever does not have the Son of God does not have life.
> [13] I write these things to you who believe in the name of the Son of God so that you may know that you have eternal life. [14] This is the confidence we have in approaching God:

that if we ask anything according to his will, he hears us. [15]
And if we know that he hears us—whatever we ask—we
know that we have what we asked of him.

When you pray to receive Jesus as Savior and Lord, God is pleased to answer that prayer!

When we receive Jesus, it is good to consider what Jesus said in Mark 8:34b-35, "Whoever wants to be my disciple must deny themselves and take up their cross and follow me. For whoever wants to save their life will lose it, but whoever loses their life for me and for the gospel will save it."

If it hasn't been clear to you yet, please hear this now: there are only two options and the consequences are eternal. We can either try to hold onto our own lives, living like the hired workers in the vineyard who tried to make their own path. Or we can lose our lives for Jesus, letting him have his rightful place as Savior and Lord. Only in receiving Jesus will we have true life.

Please know that this is an important decision – the most important one of your life! I have found that the life I live for Jesus is the one that brings true joy. That's just what Jesus promised. He told us in John 10:10 that he came so that we may have abundant life! In this new life, we have the great comfort of going through life with God! I have often said that the biggest blessing in the Bible is the blessing of God with us. Through this message of receiving Jesus as Savior and Lord, we can indeed do life with God. That's exactly what God wants for us, both now and forever!

Conclusion

Who is this Jesus? That's a question like the one people asked when they saw Jesus doing miracles and teaching from Scripture. Some were pleasantly amazed at what they saw and heard. Some were angry and wanted to stop him. Whatever the case, he caused quite a stir.

What do you say? Who is Jesus? I believe that Jesus Christ is Savior and Lord.

In this book, that's what I wanted to show you. But I know that, for some people, there are some difficult questions about who God is and whether we can trust what's in the Bible.

So the point of this book was to show you that we have very good reasons to believe in the God of the Bible and in his Son, Jesus Christ. Let me recap, quickly.

I started out in chapter one by showing you that there must be a supernatural reason why our universe exists. Like it says in Genesis 1:1, "In the beginning God created the heavens and the earth." I think that's the best answer by far. No other solution has ever made sense.

In the second chapter, I wanted to show you that the God who created the universe has further revealed himself by sending his Son, Jesus Christ. The resurrection of Jesus from the dead has stood the test of time as proof of his power over death. I showed you solid historical reasons to believe that Jesus actually rose from the dead.

Because Jesus has power over death, it makes sense that we should listen to him when he teaches us spiritual truths. In chapter three, I specifically focused on how Jesus believes the Bible to be the Word of God. To Jesus, Scripture cannot be broken (John 10:35). Since Jesus believed this about the Bible, we should listen to what the Bible says. Thankfully, the Bible clearly tells us God's plan of salvation.

In chapter four, I told you what the Bible says about salvation. We are to receive Jesus Christ. When we receive him, we should receive him for who he actually is, not as some caricature or even as someone of our own inventing. The Bible clearly portrays Jesus as Savior and Lord. As Savior, he saves us from our sins. As Lord, he is our rightful Master and we should submit to him. You can receive him as Savior and Lord simply by talking to God in prayer.

Where do we go from here?

Although receiving Jesus Christ as Savior and Lord is the most important thing you could ever do, it's really only the beginning of a life-long walk with God. After receiving Jesus, we are to keep on following him, every moment of the rest of our lives.

My favorite verse in the Bible emphasizes this ongoing relationship. Colossians 2:6 says, "So then, just as you received Christ Jesus as Lord, continue to live in him."

In that verse, we see the importance of receiving Christ Jesus as Lord. Then we see that we are to continue in him. Just as we first submitted to him as our Master, so also every moment of the rest of our lives should show that he is *still* our Master. Although that's the goal of my life, I will be the first to admit that I still fall short. When I recognize that I have done something wrong, I want to go to God in repentance as quickly as I can and then ask for the strength to walk according to his ways. That act of repentance is something I do because I want to continue walking with Jesus.

Although much could (and has!) been written about how to keep walking with Jesus, I'll leave you with four tips.

First, talk to God regularly in prayer. The Bible tells us that we are to "pray continually" (1 Thessalonians 5:17). I don't think that means we should walk around all day with our hands folded and our heads bowed. I do think it means we should continually be talking to God about the things of life, showing him that we're willing to do things his way. Talk to God throughout your day.

Second, read the Bible regularly. Again, Jesus prayed that we would be made holy by the truth of God's Word (see John 17:17). The Bible is an amazingly powerful tool which God can use to make you into the person he wants you to be. Although it may not always feel like a supernatural thing you're doing, consistently reading the Bible with a humble attitude toward God will bring life change. God will do it if you show your submission to him by reading his Word.

Third, keep in regular fellowship with other Christians. Hebrews 10:24-25 tells us we are not to give up meeting together. Things like going to church and being part of a Bible study will go a long way in helping you to continue to walk with Jesus. We were created to encourage and be encouraged by each other. I urge you to put yourself around other people who know Jesus as Lord and Savior and who listen to his Word. Find a church where they preach from the Bible. Talk to other people about your relationship with God.

Fourth, try to share God's message with others. Jesus commanded his followers to spread his message (see Matthew 28:18-20). Those of us who now know Jesus should follow that same pattern. The point of this book was to show you that God has made himself known to you. What I have tried to do in this book, you can do for others. Although God is certainly able to reveal himself to others without you, God is pleased to use you in the process. Perhaps you can use some of the truths in this book to help others know God. In doing so, I think you will become stronger in your faith.

As you walk with Jesus, God will do something powerful in you – he will confirm to you that you have become his child. You see, when you receive Jesus Christ as Savior and Lord, you enter into a relationship with God. As such, you enter into a relationship with all three members of the Trinity. There's a verse in the Bible that tells us what the third member of the Trinity, the Holy Spirit, will do to confirm us as God's children. Romans 8:16 says, "The Spirit himself testifies with our spirit that we are God's children." I believe the Holy Spirit confirms our status as God's children as we humbly walk with Jesus. God wants us to know we're on the right path.

Let me finish with one last thought. When we give our lives to Jesus, we become a new creation. The language of the Bible is that we die to our old way of life, but receive new life in Jesus. Galatians 2:20 says, "I have been crucified with Christ and I no longer live, but Christ lives in me. The life I now live in the body, I live by faith in the Son of God, who loved me and gave himself for me."

Notes

INTRODUCTION

1. R. Albert Mohler, Jr., When the Bible Speaks, God Speaks, in J. Merrick and Stephen M. Garrett (Editors), *Five Views on Biblical Inerrancy*. (Grand Rapids: Zondervan, 2013), p.45.

CHAPTER 1: CREATION REVEALS ITS CREATOR

1. Richard Dawkins, at the 10:42 mark of *The Atheist Delusion* [Motion Picture], Living Waters Publications, 2016, United States.
2. Danny Faulkner, Physics' Unsolved Energy Crisis, *Answers*, May-June 2017, Vol. 12, p.38.
3. William Lane Craig, *Reasonable Faith* (Wheaton: Crossway, 1994), p.92.
4. Danny Faulkner, Physics' Unsolved Energy Crisis, *Answers*, May-June 2017, Vol. 12, p.38.
5. Timothy Keller, *Making Sense of God* (New York: Penguin Random House, 2016), p.218.
6. Ibid., p.217.
7. Lee Strobel, *The Case for Faith* (Grand Rapids: Zondervan, 2000), p.151.
8. Ibid., p.137.
9. Ibid., p.153.
10. BBC Earth, (2013, Aug. 16), The Book of Life – Attenborough 60 Years in the Wild – BBC. Retrieved June 1, 2017, from https://www.youtube.com/watch?v=d2KVdhEDdMY.
11. Michael Behe, *Darwin's Black Box* (New York: The Free Press, 1996), p.232.
12. Lee Strobel, *The Case for Faith* (Grand Rapids: Zondervan, 2000), p.103.

CHAPTER 2: THE RESURRECTION OF JESUS SHOWS THE POWER OF GOD

1. Josh McDowell, *More Than a Carpenter* (Wheaton: Tyndale, 1977), p.89.
2. Ibid., pp.62.
3. William Lane Craig, *Reasonable Faith* (Wheaton: Crossway, 1994), p.278.
4. Ibid, p.278.
5. Lee Strobel, *The Case for Christ* (Grand Rapids: Zondervan, 2000), pp.191-204.
6. Ibid, p.200.
7. William Lane Craig, *Reasonable Faith* (Wheaton: Crossway, 1994), p.279.
8. Tacitus, *Annals*, 15.44.
9. Pliny the Younger, *Letters,* 10.96.
10. Josh McDowell, *More Than a Carpenter* (Wheaton: Tyndale, 1977), p.98.
11. *Koran* 4:157, The Everyman Library, J.M. Dent, Vermont.
12. Lee Strobel, *The Case for Christ* (Grand Rapids: Zondervan, 2000), p.247.
13. C.F.D. Moule, *The Phenomenon of the New Testament* (London: SCM Press, 1967), p.3.

CHAPTER 3: THE BIBLE IS THE WORD OF GOD

1. John Wenham, Christ's View of Scripture, in Norman Geisler (Editor), *Inerrancy*. (Grand Rapids: Zondervan, 1980), p.30.
2. D.A. Carson, *The Gospel According to John,* (Grand Rapids: Eerdmans, 1991), p.399.
3. Wayne Grudem, *Systematic Theology* (Grand Rapids: Zondervan, 1994), p.96.
4. Paul Feinberg, The Meaning of Inerrancy, in Norman Geisler (Editor), *Inerrancy*. (Grand Rapids: Zondervan, 1980), p.278.
5. Ibid, p.293.

6. John Wenham, Christ's View of Scripture, in Norman Geisler (Editor), *Inerrancy*. (Grand Rapids: Zondervan, 1980), p.17.
7. R. Albert Mohler, Jr., When the Bible Speaks, God Speaks, in J. Merrick and Stephen M. Garrett (Editors), *Five Views on Biblical Inerrancy*. (Grand Rapids: Zondervan, 2013), p.29.

8. Ibid., p.37.
9. Ibid., p.45.
10. Kevin Vanhoozer, Augustinian Inerrancy, in J. Merrick and Stephen M. Garrett (Editors), *Five Views on Biblical Inerrancy.* (Grand Rapids: Zondervan, 2013), p.202.
11. Wayne Grudem, *Systematic Theology* (Grand Rapids: Zondervan, 1994), p.73.
12. D.A. Carson, *The God Who is There*, (Grand Rapids: Baker, 2010), p.12.

CHAPTER 4: JESUS CHRIST IS SAVIOR AND LORD

1. F.F. Bruce, *Jesus: Lord & Savior*, (Downers Grove: InterVarsity, 1986), p.111.

Made in the USA
Columbia, SC
22 April 2019